NEXT-GENERATION
MEDICAL TECHNOLOGY

3D Printing and Medicine

Craig E. Blohm

ReferencePoint
Press®

San Diego, CA

© 2018 ReferencePoint Press, Inc.
Printed in the United States

For more information, contact:
ReferencePoint Press, Inc.
PO Box 27779
San Diego, CA 92198
www. ReferencePointPress.com

LIBRARY OF CONGRESS CATALOGING-IN-PUBLICATION DATA

Name: Blohm, Craig E., 1948– author.
Title: 3D Printing and Medicine/by Craig E. Blohm.
Description: San Diego, CA: ReferencePoint Press, Inc., 2018. | Series:
    Next-Generation Medical Technology | Audience: Grade 9 to 12. | Includes
    bibliographical references and index.
Identifiers: LCCN 2017034738 (print) | LCCN 2017039816 (ebook) | ISBN
    9781682823323 (eBook) | ISBN 9781682823316 (hardback)
Subjects: LCSH: Medical technology—Juvenile literature. | Three-dimensional
    printing—Juvenile literature.
Classification: LCC R855.4 (ebook) | LCC R855.4 .B56 2018 (print) | DDC
    610.28/4--dc23
LC record available at https://lccn.loc.gov/2017034738

CONTENTS

IMPORTANT EVENTS IN THE HISTORY OF 3D PRINTING

2001
Anthony Atala transplants the first 3D-printed organ, a bladder, into a patient.

1988
Engineer Scott Crump develops fused deposition modeling, a process that uses a heated plastic filament to build up 3D objects layer by layer.

1989
Carl Deckard receives a patent for his selective laser sintering 3D printing process.

| 1980 | 1985 | 1990 | 1995 | 2000 |

1980
Hideo Kodama publishes a paper in Japan describing the basic techniques for three-dimensional (3D) printing.

2002
The first miniature 3D-printed kidney is created.

1983
Engineer Charles Hull invents stereolithography and creates the first 3D-printed object: a small plastic cup.

1986
Hull forms the company 3D Systems to market the first commercial 3D printer, the SLA-1.

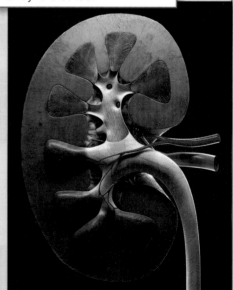

2005
Adrian Bowyer inaugurates the RepRap Project, an effort to make 3D printers more widely available.

2010
Organovo creates the first fully bioprinted blood vessels.

2007
The Organovo company is founded to commercially print human tissues.

2013
Researchers at the University of Arizona create a prototype 3D-printed retractor, a surgical instrument used to spread tissues for better access to the operating field.

2005   **2008**   **2011**   **2014**   **2017**

2006
Thomas Boland receives a patent for a process he developed to print viable cells with an ink-jet printer.

2015
Spritam, the first 3D-printed drug, is made available to the public.

2012
An eighty-three-year-old Belgian woman receives the first 3D printed prosthetic jaw.

2014
Astronauts aboard the International Space Station create the first 3D-printed tool in space: a ratchet wrench.

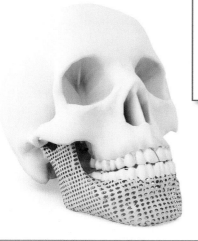

A Revolution in Medicine

When Kaiba Gionfriddo was born in October 2011, he seemed to be a normal, healthy baby. But six weeks later, while his family was at a restaurant, the infant suddenly stopped breathing and turned blue. Given CPR by his father, Kaiba was rushed to a hospital, where he was released after starting to breathe on his own. But the Gionfriddo family's nightmare was just beginning: Kaiba stopped breathing almost every day, requiring emergency artificial respiration. Doctors soon discovered that the infant had tracheobronchomalacia, a rare and usually fatal disease that caused his trachea, or windpipe, to collapse, making normal breathing impossible.

Relying on a ventilator to breathe for him, Kaiba had a slim chance of survival. Desperate for a solution, doctors at C.S. Mott Children's Hospital at the University of Michigan decided to try an experimental procedure: inserting a splint over Kaiba's windpipe to keep it open. The delicate operation succeeded, and Kaiba's lungs began filling with air. Recalls surgeon Glenn Green, "As soon as the splint was put in, the lungs started going up and down for the first time and we knew he was going to be OK."[1] The groundbreaking surgery had saved Kaiba's life, but the most remarkable aspect of the operation was the splint itself: it was made using a three-dimensional (3D) printer.

Turning Science Fiction into Science Fact

Since its invention during the 1980s, 3D printing has been employed in such areas as engineering, manufacturing, and education. Unlike standard computer printers that use ink to print documents, 3D printers use materials such as plastic, metal, and ceramics to create physical objects. These objects, which can

range from toys to industrial components, are built up by the printer layer by
layer until the item is complete. Medical
researchers eventually learned that by
using biological material for printing,
parts for the human body can be created as well. Such a scenario may seem

biomedical

relating to both biology and
medicine

like something out of a science fiction writer's imagination. Jon
Schull, the founder of e-NABLE, an organization that provides
3D-printed limbs to those in need, agrees: "We are entering an
era in which we are all remaking ourselves for the better using
emerging technologies that are science fiction–like."[2] The use of
3D printing for medical applications is turning science fiction into
science fact and is one of the fastest-growing medical technologies of the twenty-first century.

According to biomedical researcher Yu Shrike Zhang, 3D
printing "is starting to revolutionize the field of medicine by providing unprecedented flexibility and fidelity in creating volumetric

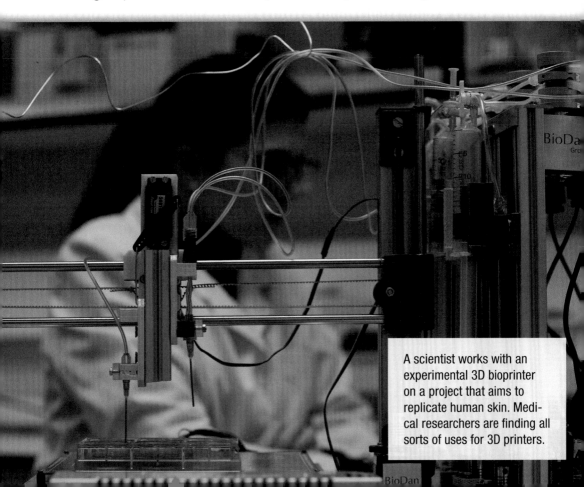

A scientist works with an
experimental 3D bioprinter
on a project that aims to
replicate human skin. Medical researchers are finding all
sorts of uses for 3D printers.

biological structures that mimic those of their native counterparts in the human body."[3] Those structures can include blood vessels, bones, and muscles as well as prostheses (artificial limbs) for accident victims and soldiers wounded in combat. Researchers in the field of pharmaceuticals are also beginning to explore the use of 3D printing to create drugs that are custom-made for individual patients. In addition, the technology is becoming a valuable tool in both the classroom and the operating room. 3D models of human organs help medical students study anatomy, and they provide a supplement to X-rays and computed tomography, or CT, scans in preparing physicians for delicate surgical procedures.

The Advantages of 3D Printing

The many advantages of 3D printing in medicine begin with improving the availability of medical solutions. Today thousands of people are on organ transplant waiting lists, and hundreds die every month while waiting for an organ. Researchers are working with 3D printers to fashion transplantable human organs. If these can be produced in large enough numbers, thousands of lives could be saved each year. 3D printing has the potential to resolve yet another problem associated with organ transplants. Organs taken from one person's body and transplanted into another are often rejected by the recipient's body. Transplant patients are required to take immunosuppressive drugs to weaken the immune system and minimize the possibility of rejection. These drugs are expensive, must be taken for life, and significantly increase the risk of infection. A 3D-printed organ made from the recipient's own cells would, in all likelihood, eliminate that problem. 3D technology can also reduce the expense of prosthetics. For example, whereas a traditional prosthesis may cost as much as $50,000 or more, the price of one created with a 3D printer may be no more than a few hundred dollars. "You can print customized prosthetics specialized for one person," notes John Rieffel, a professor of computer

> **rejection**
>
> the failure of a transplanted organ due to incompatibility with the body's immune system

science specializing in 3D printing. "This reduces cost because you produce them to order, instead of mass producing them and then sizing them."[4]

With relatively inexpensive and widely available 3D printers, third world countries may one day take advantage of medical procedures that today are too impractical or costly to implement. Locally made 3D-printed prostheses are already creating better lives for people in poor countries who suffer from injuries or birth defects. Diseases such as malaria, typhus, and cholera are found in many poverty-stricken nations. Drugs that treat or prevent such life-threatening illnesses could be economically made locally with 3D printers instead of relying on imported medicines that are expensive and difficult to obtain.

The Promise of 3D Printing in Medicine

As with most cutting-edge technologies, the future of 3D printing in medicine is difficult to predict. Researchers in the field are hopeful the technology will one day live up to its remarkable potential. "This is what technology is for," observes Schull. "Many of us are attracted to it because it's cool. But what turns out to be cool and incredibly meaningful is using it to enable a new kind of future."[5] If that future comes true, 3D printing will make health care more affordable, more personalized, and more available to people around the world.

CHAPTER 1

The Evolution of 3D Printing

Throughout history the advent of new technology has created radical changes in the ways traditional industries operate. During the fifteenth century, Johannes Gutenberg invented the movable-type printing press, opening the field of printed communication to those who previously had no access to literature. The mechanical cotton gin, invented by Eli Whitney in 1793, changed the way raw cotton was processed, revolutionizing the textile industry. During the twentieth century, such cutting-edge technologies as MRI scanning, robotic surgery, and DNA sequencing created major changes in the field of medicine. 3D printing is poised to do the same in the twenty-first century. And underlying all of these recent technological marvels is one invention: the computer.

The computer impacts not only manufacturing and medicine, but virtually every aspect of modern life. Microprocessors, the brains of any computer, are also found in nearly everything from the most sophisticated airplane to the automatic coffeemaker that sits on the kitchen counter. Combined with the Internet, computers have provided almost everyone with a gateway to a vast world of information not available at any other time in history.

Printers—which bring that information into a tangible form that can be copied, studied, and shared—have been an integral element of computer systems from the beginning. Early computer printers used tiny pins arranged in a so-called dot matrix to print characters and graphics. These printers were noisy and produced relatively crude characters. As printing technology developed over the years, ink-jet printers that shot tiny dots of ink onto paper became standard for home printing, and laser printers that featured fast printing speeds and crisp characters found their way into most business offices. Eventually printing technology became so sophisticated that even the quality of printed photographs rivaled that of pictures processed by traditional chemical methods. And yet these printers still provided only two-dimensional (2D) images. By the 1980s, designers who worked with computer-aided design (CAD) programs began to see a need for a different kind of printer.

The Development of CAD

Before any object can be built, whether it is a simple toy, an intricate motor, or a soaring skyscraper, plans must be drawn for the builders to follow. From ancient times to the twentieth century, the only way to create a plan was for designers to painstakingly draw it by hand in pencil or ink. In 1962 Ivan Sutherland, a student at the Massachusetts Institute of Technology (MIT), developed Sketchpad, the forerunner of modern CAD programs. With Sketchpad, engineers and designers could interact with their computers by drawing lines rather than typing in complicated coded instructions. "For many types of communication such as describing the shape of a mechanical part or the connections of an electrical circuit, typed statements can prove cumbersome," Sutherland wrote in his doctoral dissertation at MIT. "The Sketchpad system, by eliminating typed statements (except for legends) in favor of line drawings, opens up a new area of man-machine communication."[6]

Using Sutherland's revolutionary software, designers could for the first time create lines, curves, and geometric objects by drawing with a light pen directly onto a computer screen. The objects created could be zoomed in or out, rotated, and duplicated with ease. Sketchpad was the beginning of the now-familiar graphical user interface and gained for Sutherland the reputation as the founder of CAD. Sketchpad was developed at a time when large computers called mainframes filled rooms with control consoles and refrigerator-sized cabinets housing spinning reels of data tape. As smaller and more powerful personal computers began replacing mainframes during the 1970s and 1980s, programmers created software for these new platforms. AutoCAD was released in 1982; by 1986 it was the most popular design program used

Printing a Car

It looks almost like a Lego toy car, but the Strati is a full-size, two-seat electric automobile that became the world's first 3D-printed car in 2014. The Strati (Italian for "layers") was created by its manufacturer, Local Motors of Tempe, Arizona. The company used what is known as big area additive manufacturing, or a giant-size industrial FDM 3D printer. The car took forty-four hours to build and is made almost entirely of 3D-printed parts. The remaining parts are standard automotive components, such as the motor, battery, windshield, and wheels. Designed as an urban vehicle for use on city streets, the Strati can attain a top speed of 40 miles per hour (64 kmh).

The Strati is constructed from a plastic that is reinforced by carbon fiber, which is strong enough for its structural parts and makes the components of the car recyclable: if the Strati is in an accident, the damaged parts can be recycled and new ones printed and installed. In the future, the use of 3D printing can make customization of individual cars possible. "Because you can literally print the car any way you want," says Jay Rogers, cofounder of Local Motors, "if your family goes from two people to three—with a child—you trade in and recycle the center part of your car and all the components that outfit your family."

Local Motors is continuing its use of 3D printing in new vehicles. The LM3D Swim is a sports car designed for highway use, and the Olli is the world's first 3D-printed self-driving minibus.

Quoted in Sean Lewis, "Made in Chicago: World's First 3D Printed Electric Car," WGN-TV, September 14, 2014. www.wgntv.com.

to create 2D and 3D objects on personal computers. With AutoCAD, just about anything that could be imagined could be drawn. Designers, engineers, and inventors used AutoCAD to graphically depict their ideas in three dimensions. This marked an advance for the fields of design and engineering. But what if a computer could not only generate a plan but actually *create* the objects depicted by the plan? For that, a new type of printer was needed.

Printing in Three Dimensions

The method of using a computer printer to turn plans into real objects began with a design engineer named Charles "Chuck" Hull. In 1983 forty-four-year-old Hull was working at a job that involved using ultraviolet (UV) light to harden liquid tabletop surfaces. This process triggered an idea in Hull's mind: if the UV light could be concentrated to create thin layers of material, it might be possible to build physical objects one layer at a time. Hull explained the idea to his employer:

> I talked with the president of the company. He found it was interesting but he didn't really want to do it as a product so I agreed with him I could study this on my own time, nights and weekends in a laboratory provided by the company. So I did that, probably took several months, I don't remember how long, trying things that didn't work, finding out the first apparatus that was able actually to print 3D parts.[7]

On March 9, 1983, Hull achieved success. He called his wife, Antoinette, and asked her to come to the lab to see what he had made. "This had better be good!"[8] she admonished him. Hull's creation—a small, black plastic eye-wash cup—was not only good but also revolutionary: it was the first object ever made with the world's first 3D printer. For the printing material, Hull used liquid photopolymer, an acrylic-based material that reacts to UV light. "You have a vat of this liquid and a point of ultraviolet light, and you turn it into a solid piece of plastic,"[9] Hull explains. The solid piece is created layer by layer as the printer operates under the control of a computer program. Hull called his new manufacturing process stereolithography and was awarded a patent for his invention three years later.

stereolithography

a method of 3D printing that uses ultraviolet light to harden plastic into 3D shapes

He soon became known as the father of 3D printing, and in 2014 was inducted into the National Inventors Hall of Fame.

Rapid Prototyping with 3D Printing

By 1986 Hull had refined stereolithography to the point at which the first commercial version of his printer, the SLA-1, was ready for practical industrial use. He cofounded a company called 3D Systems to market the SLA-1 as the solution to a problem that had long bothered him. As an engineer, Hull had become impatient with the standard method of creating prototypes, which are the premanufacturing samples made for testing before a product is ready to be produced. At the time, such prototypes were created by hand, a process that could take several weeks to several months to complete. With the SLA-1, a prototype could be created in a matter of days; likewise, if a redesign was needed, it could be modified and another one quickly produced. This practice became known as rapid prototyping, and it helped manufacturers reduce the development time for new products and lower costs by identifying design problems before the expensive manufacturing stage.

prototype

the first sample of a product that can be tested and changed, if necessary, before manufacturing

Hull was not the only engineer involved in creating rapid prototyping systems. As other inventors began developing 3D printers, new ways of creating physical objects began to emerge as alternatives to Hull's UV light–based system. At the University of Texas, student Carl Deckard developed a method of 3D printing called selective laser sintering (SLS). In SLS, a laser fuses, or sinters, powdered material into solid layers that are stacked to create an object. Depending on the object to be created, the powders can be made of plastic, ceramic, metal, glass, or other substances.

Another type of 3D printing, called fused deposition modeling (FDM), was invented by Scott Crump in 1988. As an engineer, Crump, like Hull, was convinced that current prototyping methods could be improved. After making a toy frog for his daughter with a hobbyist's glue gun, Crump began tinkering with the idea of using plastic the way the glue gun used adhesive sticks. The result was a printer that could extrude heated filaments of plastic through a nozzle to build up objects, including 3D prototypes. With his wife, Lisa, Crump founded the company Stratasys to manufacture and market his FDM printers. Both FDM (now a Stratasys trademark) and FFF, or fused filament fabrication, refer to the same printing process.

These new methods of creating prototypes allowed companies to reduce the cost of creating test samples of new products. But along the way, 3D printers also pioneered a new way of manufacturing those products.

Inside a Typical Desktop 3D Printer

Industrial-size 3D printers are still more common than desktop 3D printers, but the latter have significantly improved over the last decade. The typical desktop device prints objects using a corn-based renewable plastic or other synthetic material **(1)**. To print objects, a robotic print head and extruder **(2)** operate like a hot-glue gun—layering the plastic on a build plate **(3)** that moves down as each layer of the object is printed. Using local controls **(4)**, the maker enters print settings that determine the object's size and other characteristics.

Desktop 3D printers rely on a printing method known as fused deposition modeling, or FDM. To print an object using this method, the print head first makes an outline of the object on the surface of the build plate **(A)**. The outlined shape is then filled in with a cross-hatch pattern **(B)**. The build plate moves downward as new layers are outlined and filled **(C)**, eventually resulting in the completed object.

Source: *Wall Street Journal*, "MakerBot Replicator Mini Review: 3-D Printing Comes Home," June 17, 2014. www.wsj.com.

Subtracting and Adding

There is an old tale surrounding the Italian Renaissance sculptor Michelangelo and his famous statue of the biblical David. When asked how he knew what to chip away to create his master-piece, the artist replied, "It's simple. I just remove everything that doesn't look like David."[10] Although this fictional conversation is amusing, the principle Michelangelo described applies to the modern industrial practice known as subtractive manufacturing.

As its name implies, subtractive manufacturing takes a solid piece of raw material and removes unwanted parts of the substance until what is left is the desired article. For example, numerous automobile parts, such as gears, shafts, brake components, and many other items, start out as solid blocks of steel or aluminum. Then automated drills and routers controlled by a computer eliminate unwanted metal until the part is finished. This system, also known as machining, is commonly used by auto manufacturers and numerous other industries. The traditional subtractive manufacturing process can produce precision parts economically while avoiding the problem of human error. But it requires expensive tools that do the actual machining, and it produces a lot of waste material (although much of this waste can be recycled).

With the invention of 3D printing, a new industrial process was born: additive manufacturing. In fact, the term *additive manufacturing* has now become interchangeable with *3D printing*. While subtractive manufacturing removes material, the additive process arranges successive layers of material on top of each other to build up a three-dimensional object. "What is impractical or impossible with subtractive

subtractive manufacturing

a manufacturing method whereby raw materials are drilled or cut away until what is left is the final product

additive manufacturing

a manufacturing method in which layers of raw materials are successively built up until the final product is complete; also known as 3D printing manufacturing is encouraged with additive manufacturing," says technology consultant Todd Grimm. "Additive manufacturing allows you to print virtually anything that the mind can conceive."[11]

Stereolithography was the first system of additive manufacturing, but today FDM has become the most popular method of 3D printing, especially for hobbyist use. Printing materials range from various types of plastic and metal to ceramics and even food products such as chocolate. In the additive process, a printing head, guided by computer software, heats and extrudes filaments of the chosen material through a nozzle that moves back and forth to deposit the material on a platform, or build plate. When one layer is complete, the build plate moves down a few millimeters and the next layer is deposited. This sequence continues until the final object is created, which can take anywhere from a few minutes to several days, depending on the object's size and complexity. A simple Lego-type brick, for example, may take only four or five minutes to complete, but printing a custom iPhone case might take an hour or so. Over a span of several days, objects as large as cars, boats, and even houses have been printed using special industrial-size 3D printers.

Among the many materials being used in 3D printing are plastic, metal, ceramics, and food—including chocolate and pasta. Pictured is pasta made by a 3D printer.

Industrialists and Hobbyists

By around 2005 additive manufacturing had become a practical solution for many industrial applications. The ability of high-quality printers to create large objects, accommodate a wide variety of raw materials, and employ fast printing speeds made industrial 3D printers extremely useful for rapid prototyping, creating concept models, and manufacturing end products ready to send to market. Intrigued by this new industrial process, many people became interested in making their own 3D-printed projects. But at a cost of $100,000 or more, 3D printers were out of their reach. The price point of $5,000 was considered the threshold below which ordinary consumers might consider purchasing their own 3D printer. In 2009 a company called Desktop Factory created the first 3D printer designed to be sold for just under $5,000, but production problems prevented it from going to market. Like most technological advances, however, as interest in 3D printing grew, especially with hobbyists and do-it-yourself enthusiasts, the printers became more affordable and user-friendly.

In 2005 Adrian Bowyer, a British engineering professor, started a movement called the RepRap (short for the term *replicat-*

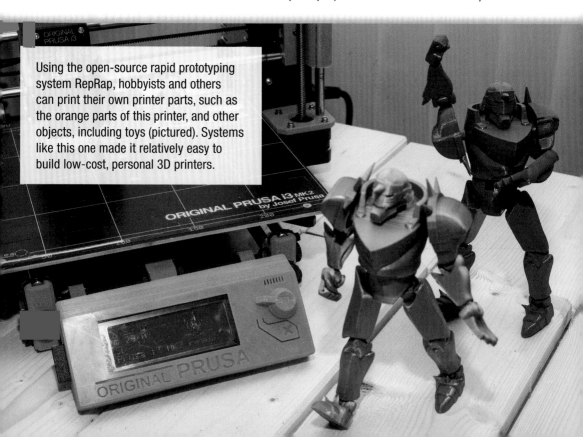

Using the open-source rapid prototyping system RepRap, hobbyists and others can print their own printer parts, such as the orange parts of this printer, and other objects, including toys (pictured). Systems like this one made it relatively easy to build low-cost, personal 3D printers.

Tools in Space

When carpenters need new hammers or screwdrivers in a hurry, they simply drop by a local store and buy them. But what if an astronaut in the International Space Station (ISS) needs a new tool? With the nearest store some 250 miles (402 km) below, another solution would be needed. Engineers at the National Aeronautics and Space Administration (NASA) looked to 3D printing to find that solution.

One of the many items aboard the ISS is a 3D printer manufactured by a company called Made in Space, Inc. To test the capability of the printer to construct tools and other components in orbit, in 2014 NASA tasked Made in Space engineers to design a simple ratchet wrench. After the design was approved, NASA e-mailed it to the ISS, the first time a design file had been sent to space. The finished wrench, which took four hours to print, measured 4.5 inches long by 1.3 inches wide (11.4 cm by 3.3 cm) and consisted of 104 layers of plastic.

Printing the plastic wrench was not done just for fun; there are real benefits to using the 3D printer on the ISS. Each pound of cargo sent to the station can cost NASA $9,000 to $40,000. In addition, astronauts must wait for a resupply ship to bring needed items, a situation that would be intolerable in an emergency.

ing rapid prototyper) Project to make 3D printers available to the masses. Bowyer's idea was to create a 3D printer that could actually reproduce itself by printing many of its own components. "I've always been interested in the idea of an artificial, self-replicating machine," Bowyer explains. "As an engineer, it was complete liberation. I could just think of something, design it and have it in my hand. It also occurred to me that we had a technology that was versatile enough to replicate itself. That's where the idea 'we'll make a 3D printer that prints itself' came from."[12]

RepRap was designed to be an open-source venture, allowing people to download the project's designs for free and thus enabling them to build a low-cost personal 3D printer. In 2008 RepRap released Darwin, its first reproducible printer. Today the RepRap community consists of thousands of hobbyist users, creating everything from toys and household goods to 3D printers for their friends. By 2017 other companies, such as Maker-Bot, Ultimaker, and XYZPrinting, were manufacturing desktop 3D printers that were available at large retailers such as Best Buy and

Walmart; they ranged in price from under $500 to around $3,500. For people who do not want to purchase a 3D printer, hundreds of public libraries across the United States have installed their own for free public use.

The World of 3D Printing

From its beginning with a laminated tabletop in Chuck Hull's lab, 3D printing has experienced remarkable growth, becoming a $5.1 billion industry in 2015. That same year more than a quarter of a million 3D desktop printers priced under $1,000 were sold worldwide. The variety of 3D-printed objects ranges from ordinary replacement parts for aging machinery to some of the most fascinating items imaginable. During Super Bowl XLVIII in 2014, players wore cleats made by 3D printers. In war-torn Afghanistan, 3D-printed models helped in the reassembly of two Buddha statues that had been destroyed by the Taliban.

But 3D printers can do so much more than make athletic shoes or archaeological models: they can improve the lives of ordinary people. For example, in 2017 Dutch researchers fashioned 3D-printed structures that help create normal facial bone growth in children born with underdeveloped eye sockets. Such medical applications may be the most challenging yet also the most rewarding use of this new technology. "With 3-D printing, the real strengths so far are complexity and customization," remarks Hull. "That's why medical applications are a natural fit in 3-D printing because all bodies are different. When you try to manufacture something for teeth, for example, they all have to be different for each patient. The same for knees and joints."[13] Today medical 3D printing is making great strides in such areas as organ replacement, prosthetics, and pharmaceuticals. According to one estimate, by 2024 the use of 3D printers in medicine is expected to be a $6 billion industry. As this cutting-edge technology grows, the health of future generations is sure to reap unimaginable benefits from the work that Hull and other visionary engineers have pioneered.

CHAPTER 2

Replacing Organs

When a vital organ becomes damaged due to disease or a congenital defect, a transplant is often the only solution. For many people, life becomes a waiting game, filled with uncertainty and anxiety. Former marathon runner Fred Knewstub almost gave up hope after waiting for a new heart for ten months. Twenty-one-year-old Joey Gill was on a kidney and liver transplant waiting list for a year and a half. Retired teacher Barbara Carpenter waited for a liver transplant for eight years. "The wait gets old because you are always on pins and needles," Carpenter said during her long delay. "I am anxious, I'm anxious to go."[14] Many such stories have happy endings, with organ transplants giving patients a new chance for life. But others do not turn out so well. According to the US Department of Health and Human Services, in 2017 about 120,000 people were on a waiting list to receive a donated organ. Every ten minutes another person was added to the list, and every day twenty-two people died waiting for a transplant that never occurred. It is difficult to harvest transplantable organs, such as the heart, lungs, kidneys, and liver; only three out of one thousand people die in a way that preserves their organs for transplanting.

There are simply not enough donors to save all of the people waiting for organs. But that may be changing. People now forced to endure the agonizing time on the transplant waiting list may ultimately be saved through the technology of 3D printing.

Engineering Organs

By the time Luke Massella was ten years old, his health had deteriorated to the point that he would became exhausted just playing with his friends. "I was really sick," Massella recalls. "I could barely get out of bed. I was missing school. It was pretty much

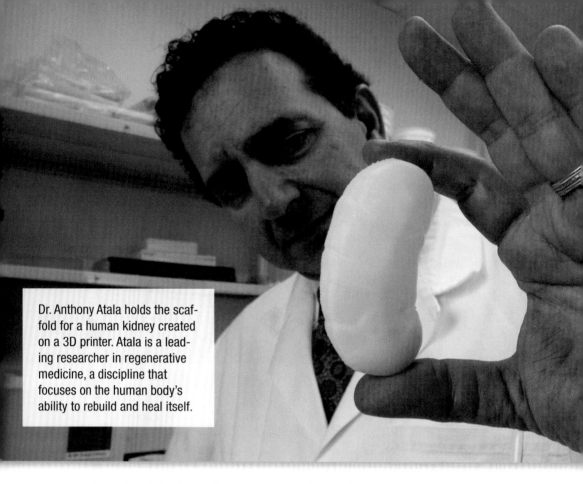

Dr. Anthony Atala holds the scaffold for a human kidney created on a 3D printer. Atala is a leading researcher in regenerative medicine, a discipline that focuses on the human body's ability to rebuild and heal itself.

miserable."[15] Massella was born with spina bifida, a birth defect in which the bones of the spine do not completely close around the spinal cord. In severe cases nerve damage occurs, which can lead to complications ranging from bladder problems to mental impairment and paralysis. In Massella's case, as is common for many sufferers of spina bifida, the size of his bladder did not keep up with his growing body. If left untreated, the disease would eventually kill him. Despite sixteen surgeries, by 2001 the damaged organ was beyond repair: what Massella needed now was a new bladder. Fortunately, there was a doctor who could build him one.

At Children's Hospital Boston, forty-seven-year-old Anthony Atala was a leading researcher in regenerative medicine, which focuses on the human body's ability to rebuild and heal itself. Atala became inspired by the way a salamander can spontaneously regrow a severed limb. "Salamanders can do it," he says. "Why can't we? Why can't humans regenerate?"[16] Atala had been conducting research since 1990 to answer that very question. By the late 1990s he was able to build bladders outside the body from a patient's own cells. After successfully testing his techniques on dogs, Atala was ready for human patients. Massella was one of seven children, ages four to nineteen, to undergo Atala's revolutionary procedure.

To construct the new bladder, Atala used a biodegradable polymer to create a scaffold, or framework, which

scaffold

a 3D framework upon which living cells are grown into a new organ

was dome-shaped and about the size of a human bladder. Then, using a 3D printer, he began coating the scaffold one layer at a time with Massella's own bladder cells, which had been harvested and grown in a laboratory petri dish. Atala describes the procedure:

> We actually take a very small piece of the bladder from the patient—less than half the size of a postage stamp. We then grow the cells outside the body, take the scaffold, coat the scaffold with the cells—the patient's own cells, two different cell types. We then put it in this oven-like device. It has the same conditions as the human body. . . . A few weeks later, you have your engineered organ that we're able to implant back into the patient.[17]

The two different types of cells used as printing material in Atala's 3D printer were deposited on the scaffold, with urothelial cells on the inside and muscle cells on the outer surface. Once printing was complete, the newly created organ was attached to Massella's diseased bladder; ultimately it took over the function of the old organ. Massella's new bladder dramatically improved his health. "I was able to be a normal kid with my friends," he says. "And because they used my own cells to build this bladder, it's going to be with me. I've got it for life, so I'm all set."[18] Massella became captain of his high school wrestling team, and in 2013 he graduated from college, all with the help of the bladder that had been specially printed for him.

"We're happy because we've gotten this far," says Atala, who continues his research at the Wake Forest Institute for Regenerative Medicine in Winston-Salem, North Carolina. "But we realize at the same time that there are many other tissues and many other challenges ahead of us, so we have to keep focused and keep the course."[19] One of those challenges was finding a way to keep 3D-printed organs alive.

Tissue Engineering

The bladder that Atala implanted into Massella was essentially very simple: a hollow organ made up of only two types of cells. This made the job of printing the organ, however revolutionary, a relatively straightforward process. But the structure of other organs in the human body, such as the liver, heart, and kidneys, is not quite as simple. Before researchers could progress toward the goal of creating these organs, they needed a way to create the blood vessels that would keep the organs alive.

At the University of Missouri–Columbia in 2004, biological physicist Gabor Forgacs and his research team were focused on using a printer to create tubular structures that could serve as blood vessels. "A large part of the body is made of tubes," notes Forgacs. "We can now make 3-D hollow biological tubes and organ modules. . . . The next step is the construction of functional organ modules, prepared outside of the living organism and then implanted into the organism."[20] Forgacs's printer contained three print heads that deposited tiny spheroids, or dots, of bioink onto a sheet of gelatin called biopaper. The bioink consisted of clusters of cells called cell aggregates, which may be thought of as tiny pieces of tissue. The biopaper, according to Forgacs, "is a material that mimics what we have in our body between the organs, that surrounds the organs. It's called the extracellular matrix. Cells love it."[21] Once the first layer of bioink was deposited, another layer of biopaper was printed; the process continued until the tubular structure was complete.

spheroids

tiny globes of living tissue deposited by a 3D printer

Forgacs's technology became the basis for a bioprinting company called Organovo. Established in 2007 with Forgacs as its scientific founder, Organovo's goal was to commercially print human tissues to replace damaged or diseased tissues as well as to use in medical research. In 2009 Organovo was awarded a grant

How Bioprinting Works

Bioprinting is the use of living organisms, such as cells, as raw material for 3D printing. The process works like this: **(1)** Cells are placed into a growth medium where they will multiply. Clustered cells, or aggregates, are used to form bioink. **(2)** Bioprinter cartridges consisting of a syringe and long extrusion nozzle are filled with the bioink. **(3)** The bioprinter layers the bioink in precise amounts and patterns. A separate nozzle deposits a water-based substance called hydrogel between these layers, creating a temporary mold around the cells. **(4)** The mold is removed once the printed tissue has grown and matured. **(5)** The printed tissue is now ready for use in research or as transplant material.

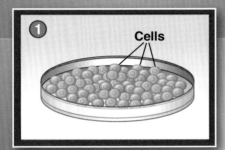

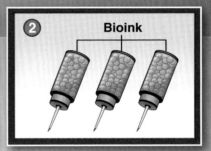

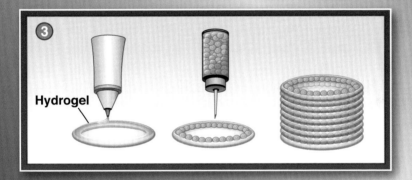

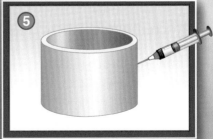

Source: *Economist*, "Bioprinters: Printing a Bit of Me," March 8, 2014. www.economist.com.

from the National Institutes of Health for the creation of bioprinted blood vessels. Two years later its research led to the creation of a 3D-printed blood vessel that in the future could be used in such procedures as heart surgery. Instead of bypassing a clogged blood vessel with a vein taken from another location in the body, as is the current method, the printed vessel could be used, making the surgery less invasive for the patient.

Although these blood vessels are a step forward in 3D printing biotechnology, it takes more than a single vessel to keep an organ alive. So Harvard University researchers learned how to create an entire vascular network within the extracellular matrix.

The Vascular Tree

In a laboratory at Harvard University's Wyss Institute for Biologically Inspired Engineering, a 3D printer sits on a 1.5 ton (1.4 t) block of granite. The heavy base is necessary to stabilize the printer for the delicate work of printing biological tissues that may one day lead to the creation of complete organs. "Most of the efforts in tissue printing," explains Jennifer Lewis, a researcher in materials engineering, "have been able to print cells and extracellular matrix, but they haven't been able to include the vascular network, and that limits the complexity of the tissues you can print." In 2013 Lewis and her research team began working toward overcoming that limit. "Our first step is to explore what we can harness through 3D printing, and what we can couple with biology to create the next generation of tissue architectures," Lewis says. "We want . . . [eventually] to be able to create more complex tissues that might even be able to be used for tissue regeneration and repair."[22]

Lewis needed a way to create tiny tubes, or microchannels, within an extracellular matrix that could carry blood to nourish the tissue. In 2011, while Lewis was at the University of Illinois, she had developed a new kind of ink with a unique property. The ink had a thick, paste-like consistency at room temperature but, contrary to what might be expected, liquefied when cooled to near freezing. She called her innovation "fugitive ink" and put it to use in 3D printing of vascular tissues.

One of the difficulties in creating the thicker tissues necessary for building organs is the problem of keeping these tissues alive. Nature solved this problem by permeating biological organs with networks of blood vessels, called vascular trees. Lewis came up with a method using a 3D printer and her new ink that would artificially re-create what nature formed on its own. The process begins by printing a small block of material using fibroblasts, the cells making up the extracellular matrix that gives structure to a biological organism. Within that block a network of channels, branching out like a tree, is created with fugitive ink. Once the printing phase is complete, the block is cooled to the point where the fugitive ink liquefies, allowing it to be removed by suction. The end result is tissue containing channels similar to a natural vascular tree, through which blood can flow.

One small piece of tissue in itself, however, does not make an organ. Hearts, livers, and kidneys are incredibly complex organs;

Creating Cells with an Ink-Jet Printer

When the printer was finished with its job, Thomas Boland looked down at the result. His initials, printed just a moment before, were easy to recognize in the printout: an off-white *TB* appeared on the paper. Although the printout itself did not look remarkable, it was the first time that something had been printed not with ink but with proteins, which are the building blocks of life.

In 2000, when Boland was an assistant professor of bioengineering at Clemson University in South Carolina, he wondered if he could use biological materials instead of ink in his lab's Lexmark ink-jet printer. After removing the ink from a cartridge, he filled it with collagen, a protein found in skin, bones, blood vessels, and other structures—the most abundant protein in the human body. Then, with the aid of a word processing program, Boland's initials rolled off the printer, the first objects to be printed with living proteins. With this experience behind him, Boland began using other materials as bioink, including *E. coli* bacteria and cells from rats and hamsters. The success of these experiments led Boland to apply for a patent for his innovation in 2003. In 2006 Boland's patent for ink-jet printing of viable cells was awarded. Since then, thousands of people have benefited from his pioneering work.

the ultimate goal of bioprinting is to be able to create such organs. Lewis and her research team have made important strides toward that goal by 3D printing proximal tubules, which are tiny serpentine structures inside a kidney that helps that organ function. The proximal tubules are a part of the kidney's nephrons, the basic structural elements of the organ, and Lewis prints them in a manner similar to the creation of blood vessels. According to Lewis, "We're breaking the nephron down into these modular units, laying the foundation for the building blocks. We're testing the structure and function of the modular units with ultimately the goal of trying to assemble a single nephron."[23] The fact that a human kidney contains more than 1 million nephrons makes it clear that a fully functional 3D-printed kidney is still many years away.

bioprinting

the use of living organisms, such as cells, as raw material for 3D printing

Rebuilding the Body

If the potential for 3D printing a variety of body parts seems endless, the road toward one day creating body parts at will is a long one. But the first steps are already being made in research labs both in the United States and abroad. In China, a three-year-old named Han Han had been born with hydrocephalus, a fluid buildup in the brain that caused her skull to swell to four times its normal size. "CT [computed tomography] results showed that Han Han's brain was filled 80 percent with water," recalls Dr. Bo of the Second People's Hospital of Hunan Province. "If she was not sent to hospital for treatment, Han Han would not have survived the summer."[24] In 2015 doctors used a 3D printer to construct three titanium implants to replace the top of the toddler's skull—a first in medical history. The implants were installed during a seventeen-hour operation, after which Han Han was expected to make a full recovery.

In Spain, scientists have been working with 3D printed skin. The skin is the body's largest organ and, as the protective outer layer, it can suffer from burns, lacerations, and other traumas. Rebuilding burned skin is a painful procedure that requires taking skin from uninjured parts of the body to graft onto the burned area. The Spanish scientists have successfully used 3D-printed skin, which incorporates the multilayered structure of actual human skin, to create grafts for burn victims.

In the United States, scientists from the Wake Forest Institute for Regenerative Medicine are collaborating with US military researchers. The goal of this joint project is to develop a 3D printing technology that can print healthy skin directly onto burn wounds, as opposed to printing a separate piece of skin and then placing it onto the burned area.

Rebuilding the heart is another area in which 3D printing is being studied. Diseased heart valves can cause serious health problems, including stroke, heart failure, or cardiac arrest. At Denver University (DU) in Colorado, researchers are creating heart valves using the BioBot 1, a $10,000 3D printer that can print a valve in about twenty-two minutes. "We're really trying to take what's become an accessible tool," says Ben Stewart, a graduate research assistant at DU, "and use the most sophisticated thinking that we can to create something that will benefit all people."[25] Children who

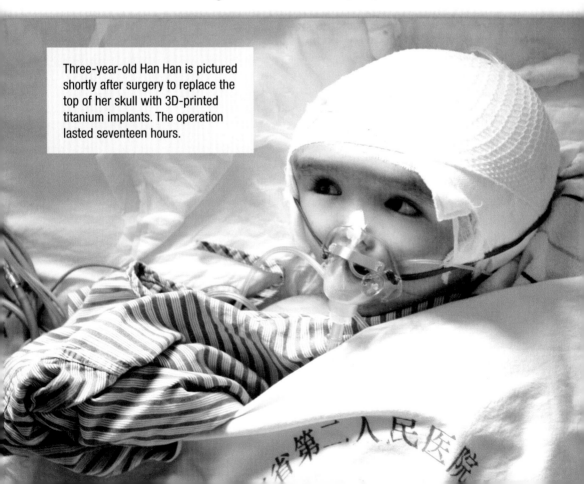

Three-year-old Han Han is pictured shortly after surgery to replace the top of her skull with 3D-printed titanium implants. The operation lasted seventeen hours.

are born with congenital heart valve defects, for whom traditional valve prostheses are often not an option, will be among those who benefit the most. As Ali Azadani, director of the DU Cardiac Biomechanic Lab, explains, "That (prosthetic) valve cannot grow as the child grows. So those patients typically need to go through multiple surgeries for their aortic valve. That's very invasive, and that's not the best approach. By designing tissue engineered valves, we can implant a valve in the heart that can grow with the child."[26]

Implanting these valves in humans, as well as building complete 3D-printed hearts, is still years away. In the meantime, research on other 3D-printed organs is growing. 3D-printed ovaries have been successfully implanted in mice. In addition, research continues into bone implants that can help heal fractured limbs. And so-called miniorgans, which are small cellular patches, may be used to repair cardiac tissue damaged by a heart attack.

The Next Step: 4D

Now that 3D printing is established as a cutting-edge technology for making organs and for other medical applications, what could be a more logical step forward than four-dimensional (4D) printing? "The idea behind 4D printing," says Skylar Tibbits, founder of the Self-Assembly Lab at the Massachusetts Institute of Technology, "is that you take multi-material 3D printing—so you can deposit multiple materials—and you add a new capability, which is transformation . . . the parts can transform from one shape to another shape directly on their own." With this new technology, heat, gravity, moisture, or other stimuli cause a 3D-printed object to change its shape. The key is embedding a code into the object during printing; that code describes how it should transform itself.

What does this mean for the medical field? A 4D-printed cardiac stent, for example, could be made to expand itself when placed in an artery instead of having the surgeons inflate it with a balloon, as is current practice. Or an implanted drug could be released into the bloodstream when a person's temperature rises due to infection. The future may see an implanted organ that can change its characteristics when acted on by biological, physiochemical, or nutritional factors.

Whenever a cutting-edge technology is invented, another advancement nearly always follows. Practical 4D technology may be far in the future, but in the minds of creative thinkers, it is already just around the corner.

Skylar Tibbits, "The Emergence of 4D Printing," TED Talk, February 2013. www.ted.com.

Ethical Concerns

3D-printed tissues and organs have the ability to make life better for thousands of people who suffer from injury or disease. But not everyone who needs this technology will be able to take advantage of it. Pete Basiliere, a researcher in additive manufacturing, expresses his concern about where medical 3D printing may be headed: "Three-D bioprinting facilities with the ability to print human organs and tissue will advance far faster than general understanding and acceptance of the ramifications of this technology. These initiatives are well-intentioned, but raise a number of questions that remain unanswered."[27]

Researchers like Basiliere and others who study medical ethics wonder who will benefit from new 3D-printed hearts, kidneys, and other organs. The cost of such technology will likely be high—at least initially. They wonder if those costs will limit these potentially lifesaving technologies to only those who can afford them. And they wonder if demand will outstrip supply, possibly leading to a black market in which organs of questionable quality are sold. Some even wonder if athletes will seek out 3D printed organs to gain an advantage over their competitors—a move that might be construed as cheating. These are just some of the ethical concerns that have been raised and will likely be discussed in the years to come.

The creation of fully functioning 3D-printed organs is still years, perhaps decades, in the future. But the technology is here today, and it is advancing at an astounding pace. Researchers look forward to the day when organ transplant waiting lists are a thing of the past, the sick can receive personalized medicine, and every child born with a birth defect has the opportunity to lead a normal life.

CHAPTER 3

Creating New Body Parts

Karissa Mitchell was born without her right hand and most of her wrist. But after her mother reached out to a group of college students, Karissa received a remarkable gift. In 2016, eight students at Siena College in New York used 3D printing to create a new arm for Karissa. The nine-year-old was delighted when she saw that the design of the ice-blue arm was inspired by her favorite movie, *Frozen*. Karissa's arm is just one example of how 3D printing has ushered in a new era in the science of prosthetics.

Early Prosthetics

Prosthetics is the branch of medicine dealing with the replacement of a missing body part with an artificial structure, known as a prosthesis. People missing arms, legs, hands, fingers, or other body parts due to injury or disease benefit from the art and science of prosthetics. From ancient times through the sixteenth century, prosthetics remained rather crude, with missing arms or legs replaced by limbs made of iron or wood. Not surprisingly, wars throughout history produced a great need for prostheses to replace limbs lost in battle. By the time the American Civil War was raging, prostheses began featuring hinged joints that improved mobility—a little.

The twentieth century brought two devastating world wars and more advances in prosthetics. These included the use of lightweight materials such as plastic, aluminum, and carbon fiber; custom sockets designed for individual patients; and control of prostheses with microprocessors. These modern innovations have made prostheses more comfortable and more versatile, but they are also fairly costly. Now 3D printing is ushering in the next step in the evolution of prosthetics: artificial limbs that weigh less and cost less, which means they are more readily available to people from all corners of the globe.

According to the World Health Organization, as of 2017 some 30 million people around the world would benefit from having a prosthesis. In addition to people born with physical deformities, these candidates include individuals who have been injured in natural disasters, accidents, and wars. 3D printing may hold the key to providing them with the artificial limbs they need.

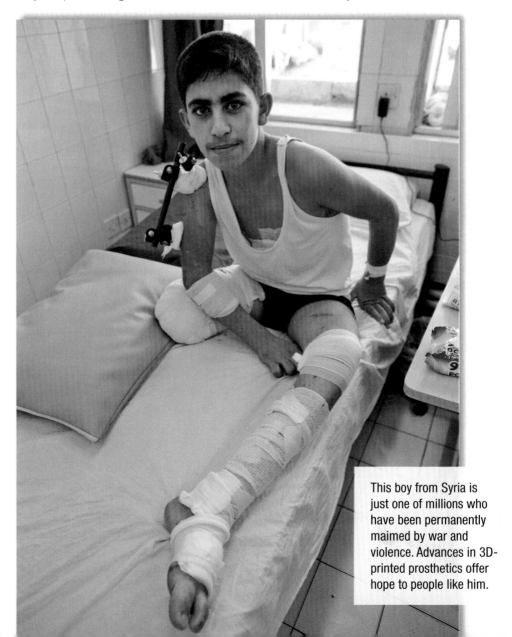

This boy from Syria is just one of millions who have been permanently maimed by war and violence. Advances in 3D-printed prosthetics offer hope to people like him.

Bionic Arms

In 2010 a magnitude 7.0 earthquake devastated the Caribbean nation of Haiti, causing widespread death and destruction. Twenty-year-old Danis Exulise lost her left arm after being trapped for hours in the rubble of her house. In 2016 Exulise received a 3D-printed arm from a New York–based company called Create Prosthetics. It was the first medical-grade device of its kind, which means that it met strict government guidelines for the safety and effectiveness of medical devices. Weighing about 2 pounds (0.9 kg), or about half the weight of a traditional prosthetic arm, its simple construction allows Exulise to grasp and hold objects. As Jeff Erenstone, Create's founder, explains, "We have found a niche that a 3D-printed prosthetic arm fills very well. Other prosthetic arms may be more functional, but our arm is very attractive and easy to become accustomed to."[28] The company now makes prosthetic kits that enable the creation of prosthetic arms, hands, and fingers.

Although the Create Prosthetics kits are used by specialists, prosthetic devices are becoming available to anyone via the Internet.

The Mummy's Toe

The use of 3D technology to make prosthetics is the latest advancement in the long history of making artificial limbs. But modern scientists have made a discovery that shows how far back these efforts go.

In 2000, archaeologists discovered an artificial big toe attached to the mummy of a woman in a tomb near the ancient Egyptian city of Thebes. Made of wood and leather, the toe has three joints for ease of movement and shows signs of use. It is estimated to have been made between 950 and 710 BCE, making it the world's oldest example of a prosthetic. The toe belonged to Tabaketenmut, the daughter of an Egyptian priest, who likely lost her toe to diabetes.

To find out if Tabaketenmut's prosthesis improved her ability to walk, researchers asked two volunteers who had also lost a big toe to test a replica of the prosthesis. Walking tests were performed and data was collected from cameras and pressure-sensitive mats. The artificial toe helped the volunteers walk in reproductions of leather Egyptian sandals, and both declared the prosthesis comfortable.

Tabaketenmut is the first known person to have benefited from the science of prosthetics. Researchers today who use 3D printing to create modern prostheses are continuing a great tradition of helping people to regain functions lost to injury or disease.

Fifty-three-year-old José Delgado Jr. has lived his entire life without a left hand, the result of a birth defect. Over the years he has tried several types of prostheses, with varying degrees of success. One of these was a $42,000 myoelectric arm, which operates via electrical impulses generated from his muscle and nerve activity.

Delgado noted several drawbacks with this prosthesis, including the fact that not all of the fingers moved for gripping. He also experienced some difficulty with the arm while driving.

In 2014 he had an opportunity to be fitted with a 3D-printed hand constructed with the same kind of plastic that Lego bricks are made of, a popular and inexpensive 3D printing material. Jeremy Simon, a former computer consultant now specializing in 3D printing, built the hand—known as the Cyborg Beast—for about fifty dollars from a free online design. It relies on a mechanical system of wires to move the fingers when Delgado bends his wrist.

When Delgado evaluated the Cyborg Beast against his other prosthesis, he found that he prefers the new hand while he is on the job, which involves lifting boxes. "The 3D [hand] has all the functions of the fingers," he notes, "so I like that better. . . . When I bend my wrist I get enough grip on the bottom of the boxes."[29]

Jorge Zuniga, a research scientist at the University of Nebraska–Omaha, invented the Cyborg Beast. "You can do anything with 3D printing," he says. "We believe it will revolutionize the prosthetics field. It will lower the costs worldwide and gives engineers, patients and doctors the chance to modify prosthetic hands as they want."[30] By 2017 more than five hundred people in countries around the world were using the Cyborg Beast.

Help for People Who Need It Most

The dramatically reduced cost, speed of building, and ease of customization for individual patients make 3D-printed prostheses especially suitable for use in third world countries where war often turns bystanders into amputees. Children are especially vulnerable in dangerous hot spots such as Afghanistan, Syria, and Iraq, a situation that has prompted numerous organizations to provide 3D-printed limbs for the young victims of war.

Fourteen year old Daniel Omar lives in the war-torn region of South Kordofan in the northern African nation of Sudan. For years, armed conflict there produced frequent bombing raids. One day when Daniel heard planes overhead, he desperately looked for cover. Finding nowhere to hide, he wrapped his arms around the nearest tree, hoping it would shield him. Although his body was protected from the bomb's blast, his arms were so badly injured that they had to be amputated. Without arms, Daniel could not do even the simplest tasks of everyday life.

Film producer Mick Ebeling read a magazine article about Daniel and was inspired to act. In 2013 Ebeling established the Daniel Project, an effort to provide 3D-printed prostheses to Daniel and to thousands of other individuals who had lost limbs to the violence in Sudan. Ebeling assembled a team that would help put his vision into action. "I came to Sudan," he explains, "with 3D printers, laptops, spools of plastic and the goal to print Daniel an arm." In November 2013 Daniel received a prosthetic arm, which enabled him to once more feed himself and feel more like a normal person. Before returning home, Ebeling trained local people in how to operate the 3D printers, forming a prosthetics lab that continues to turn out 3D-printed arms. Says Ebeling, "We're hopeful that other children and adults in other regions of Africa, as well as other continents around the globe, will utilize the power of this new technology for similar beginnings."[31]

Not only is 3D printing helping people with missing hands or arms, but it also is beginning to have an impact on people who were born without legs or feet or who lost them during wars or accidents. In 2015 a team of Canadian researchers from the University of Toronto created the first 3D-printed leg socket for a young Ugandan woman's traditional prosthesis. The most critical part of an artificial limb, the socket must be custom fitted to each patient, which is an expensive and time-consuming process. It can take days to produce a socket with traditional methods that rely on plaster casts and require multiple fitting sessions; however, the process is simplified with 3D printing. "The 3D technology we've introduced in Uganda cuts this work down to as little as six hours," explains researcher Matt Ratto. "You can make exact adjustments, rather than guessing like we do with the manual method."[32]

The work Ratto and his team pioneered in Uganda is applicable to the rest of the world as well. "It isn't so much a developed-world technology being redeployed to a developing world context, it's exactly the reverse," he says. "Everything we're learning through this project can be used in developed countries to help produce prosthetics more efficiently and affordably."[33]

Replacing Legs

The use of 3D printing of artificial legs and feet is a relatively new area of prosthetics. Lower limb prostheses must bear the weight of a body, and this feat is easier to accomplish with traditional prostheses than with 3D printing. But advances are being made in many countries around the world.

Denise Schindler is a German paralympic athlete who lost her right leg below the knee in an accident at the age of three. She

German paralympic cyclist Denise Schindler shows off her various artificial legs. She wore a high-tech 3D-printed prosthetic leg in the 2016 Paralympic Games—and won silver and bronze medals in her events.

won a silver medal as a cyclist in the 2012 Paralympic Games, but she experienced abrasions and pain from her traditional prosthesis. Realizing that she needed something better for the 2016 games, Schindler began working with software company Autodesk to design a new 3D-printed leg. "This is going to be the world's first prosthetic at the Paralympics that has been 3D printed," designer Paul Sohi said in 2016. "We're at a stage technology-wise to initiate a paradigm shift in this industry."[34]

Two years of design and prototyping work went into the creation of the leg, which is made of polycarbonate, a high-strength plastic. It took a mere forty-eight hours to print the aptly named Real Racing Leg, which weighs just 1.8 pounds (0.8 kg) and cost $2,650—about one-fifth the cost of Schindler's regular prosthesis. Sohi envisions a strong future for 3D-printed limbs. "Because everything is digitally distributable," he says, "you can democratize the manufacturing and you can build prosthetics anywhere in the world. This is very much the future of prosthetics."[35] In the 2016 Paralympic Games, Schindler won silver and bronze medals, with no discomfort from her 3D-printed leg. She and Sohi have begun working on developing a leg suitable for walking.

polycarbonate

a strong synthetic thermoplastic used in the making of prostheses

A 3D-printed walking leg has already been created in the United Arab Emirates (UAE). After living in pain for eighteen years, the result of being thrown from a horse, British citizen Belinda Gatland had her left leg amputated at the age of forty. Traditional prosthetics helped her walk, but they were expensive and had to be replaced often to accommodate her active lifestyle. After moving to the city of Dubai in the UAE for her husband's job, she was fitted with a 3D-printed leg in 2017 as part of a trial from the Dubai Health Authority. Creating the leg was a truly international endeavor, with parts being made in Germany and Bulgaria, which were then shipped to Dubai for the final fitting on Gatland.

Printed in light blue plastic with decorative cutouts, the prosthesis is eye-catching as well as functional. "It is very comfortable," she says. "I could put it on straight out of the machine, rather than go through casting, a test socket and the many different consultations that are needed. There isn't much I can't do with this leg."[36] That includes doing what she loves most—riding horses.

Bionic Restoration

Prostheses are an obvious benefit for people without arms, legs, hands, or feet. However, such devices will not help those who have lost the ability to walk or perform other ordinary tasks due to spinal cord injuries. Many researchers are now looking to 3D printing to provide mobility where such capabilities have been lost.

After Amanda Boxtel suffered a skiing accident in 1992 that paralyzed her from the waist down, doctors told her that she would never walk again. That prediction was dashed twenty-two years later when two companies, 3D Systems and Ekso Bionics, partnered to create for Boxtel the first robotic exoskeleton employing 3D technology. Using 3D scanners, the shape and contours of Boxtel's body were converted to digital format,

The Perfect Smile

A person's smile can be an important factor in social and business situations but, perhaps more importantly, it can influence how people feel about themselves. Metal braces have long been the standard solution for correcting misaligned teeth, but they can be unsightly, difficult to keep clean, and require constant maintenance. To address these problems, in 1999, a company called Align Technology created clear plastic dental straighteners under the name Invisalign. Unlike metal braces, the aligners are virtually invisible and can be removed when eating and brushing teeth. They are worn up to twenty-two hours per day; new aligners are provided every two weeks to progressively move teeth to their proper position in the mouth. With 4 million patients as of September 2016, Align Technology relies on 3D printing to print more than 175,000 straighteners per day, more than their competitors print in a year.

After researching commercial aligners, college student Amos Dudley decided to try making his own plastic aligners with the help of a Stratasys 3D printer. He found that they were more comfortable than his former metal braces and actually helped correct his misaligned teeth. Still, Dudley recommends leaving the process to professional orthodontists.

which was then used to 3D print a personalized exoskeleton. Custom fitting the robotic suit was critical in preventing bruises, which a paralyzed person cannot feel but can lead to dangerous infections. "We had to be very specific with the design," says Scott Summit of 3D Systems, "so we never had 3D-printed parts bumping into bony prominences, which can lead to abrasions."[37] With 3D printing, these components were made with an intricate perforated pattern that permitted them to be strong, lightweight, and flexible yet allowed Boxtel's skin to breathe.

actuator

a device that uses myoelectric energy to control the movements of a prosthesis

After 3D Systems printed the parts for the exoskeleton, Ekso Bionics provided the mechanical actuators that allow the device, which is attached to Boxtel's back and lower extremities, to stand and walk. These are, of course, the principal reasons for building such a device. But for Boxtel, life with her 3D-printed exoskeleton goes beyond mere mobility:

> An exoskeleton can become so much more than enabling a person to walk again. It can become an art form of moving sculptured beauty reproduced from a person's own blueprint. A paralyzed man or woman can look forward to being beautiful, standing tall and walking again in the ultimate fashion statement . . . a 3D printed exoskeleton that reflects who they are on the inside.[38]

Although most people may not think of an artificial limb as a fashion statement, a person's appearance can play a role in strengthening, or diminishing, self-esteem. 3D printing is helping people who must cope with physical disfigurements that have a profound effect on their quality of life.

A New Outlook on Life
Nine-year-old Dallan Jennet of the Marshall Islands in the Pacific Ocean was the unfortunate victim of an accident with a live power line. The accident severely burned his face and destroyed

his nose. With help from a GoFundMe campaign and a nonprofit organization called Canvasback Missions, in 2015 Dallan's family was put in touch with Dr. Tal Dagan. A New York facial reconstruction surgeon, Dagan led a team that gave Dallan a new 3D-printed nose. The nose prosthesis was printed by Oxford Performance Materials, a company that specializes in materials technology and additive manufacturing in the biomedical, aerospace, and industrial markets. In a delicate sixteen-hour operation, the prosthesis was attached to Dallan's face and then covered with his own skin to more closely resemble a normal human nose. It was the first time such an operation was performed. "This procedure may be a breakthrough in facial reconstruction," Dagan remarks, "because the patient will never have to deal with the standard issues of transplantation, such as tissue rejection or a lifetime of immunosuppressive therapies."[39] The implant has restored Dallan's sense of smell and taste and, perhaps most importantly, given him a chance to live a happy and normal life.

Sometimes people like Dallan must wait years for a new technology that addresses their condition. But when it comes, it is well worth the wait. In Australia, Coleen Murray received a new 3D-printed ear fifty-five years after she lost her left ear in an automobile accident. The ear, made of silicone, was created to look

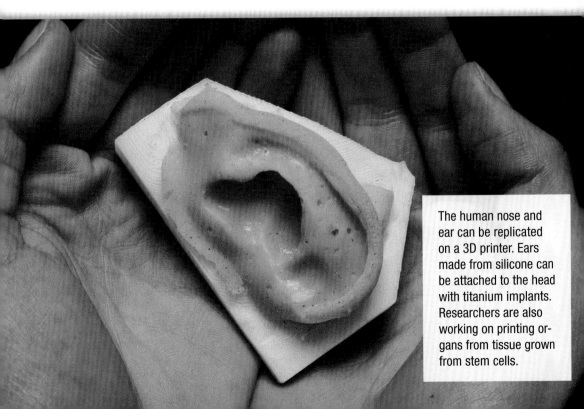

The human nose and ear can be replicated on a 3D printer. Ears made from silicone can be attached to the head with titanium implants. Researchers are also working on printing organs from tissue grown from stem cells.

idontical to hor right car for a completely natural look. Attached with titanium implants, the new ear matches her skin tone with just a touch of makeup. While many 3D-printed implants are, like Murray's, made of medical-grade silicone, researchers are also working with stem cells from a patient's own body. Stem cells, which can develop into many different types of cells in the body, can be used to print such tissue as muscles and cartilage, which compose an ear.

Not all 3D-printed prostheses are visible to the outside world. With an aging population, hip replacement surgeries are becoming commonplace. Traditional replacement hips are made of solid titanium for strength—and that creates a problem. The joint is so strong that it absorbs the stress of walking, leaving the connecting bone weaker and ultimately causing pain and, often, the need for further surgery. At McGill University in Montreal, Canada, researchers have developed a new 3D-printed hip implant that can alleviate this problem. Made of titanium in a latticework pattern, the implant fools the bone to which it is attached into accepting the implant as a part of the bone itself. This encourages the real bone to continue to grow and strengthen, giving the hip joint a longer life.

In India, doctors created 3D-printed vertebrae for a woman whose backbone was deteriorating, a condition that would ultimately lead to paralysis. Doctors created several titanium vertebrae using an advanced metal 3D printer and then implanted them in the patient during a ten-hour operation. "It was a very complex surgery," recalls surgeon V. Anand Naik, "and the patient's condition was deteriorating by the day. It would not have been possible to do it without 3D printing technology."[40] Less than two weeks after the operation, the patient could again walk without constant pain.

Whether outwardly visible or hidden within the body, 3D-printed prostheses hold the promise of a better life for people who have suffered from traumatic injuries or debilitating illnesses. One day, 3D printers may become as common in hospitals as patient monitors, CT scanners, and electrocardiograph machines.

CHAPTER 4

Printing Pharmaceuticals

The business of developing, manufacturing, and marketing drugs is one of the largest industries in the world. The International Federation of Pharmaceutical Manufacturers & Associations, an industry trade group, estimates that by the year 2020 pharmaceuticals will grow into a $1.43 trillion industry. Just the research necessary to create a new drug costs pharmaceutical companies nearly $150 billion per year. And the process is a lengthy one, taking anywhere from ten to fifteen years for a company to define a medical need, conduct research, perform clinical trials, and receive government approval before bringing a drug to market. The laboratories, factories, and skilled personnel needed to create a drug are all part of the expense of bringing people the medicine that will cure an ailment or relieve chronic suffering. But 3D printing is poised to make inroads into the pharmaceutical industry.

How Drugs Are Made

Drug manufacturing begins with the development phase, in which a chemical compound, or active pharmaceutical ingredient (API), is identified. The API is then subjected to numerous tests to determine whether it is safe and whether it treats the condition it is intended for. These tests also assess possible side effects. The manufacturer also determines in what form the drug should be given to patients—whether it should be in tablet, capsule, or liquid form, for instance.

Production of a drug requires many additional steps. To create a tablet, for example, a powder form of the API is mixed with a nonmedicinal filler called an excipient. The excipient increases the bulk of the drug and assists with the proper absorption of the medicine in the body. The resulting mixture is deposited into numerous molds, or dies, in a large press that uses between two and five tons of pressure to compact the substance into a tablet-shaped solid. This automated procedure can produce thousands of pills per minute. The pills are then sprayed with a coating mixture that prevents them from crumbling and makes them easier for the patient to swallow. Finally, the newly created drugs are sent to a packaging machine that deposits them into bottles or in blister packs to be delivered to pharmacies.

The process of producing pharmaceuticals is a highly automated, high-volume industry. In 2016 more than 4 billion pre-

The highly automated pharmaceuticals production process (pictured) might soon be undergoing change. Several companies are working with 3D printing technology to develop drugs that are easier to swallow or that better fit an individual patient's needs.

scriptions were filled at US retail pharmacies, an average of more than twelve prescriptions for every man, woman, and child in the United States. And that does not take into account drugs supplied in hospitals, nursing homes, and urgent care centers. Only a relatively few companies have the monetary and manufacturing resources to succeed in this high-stakes, high-dollar industry. But the development of 3D printers has created the potential for an industry-wide change in the way drugs are manufactured and distributed.

3D Printing Pharmaceuticals

With all the specialized equipment currently used by pharmaceutical manufacturers, is there a place on the factory floor for 3D printers? A company named Aprecia Pharmaceuticals thinks so. In fact, the company was founded in 2003 with the goal of using 3D printing technology exclusively to produce unique formulations of pharmaceuticals.

Many people, especially children and the elderly, have difficulty swallowing medications in pill form. Studies have shown that people with such problems are likely to skip taking a medication, which compromises the overall effectiveness of a treatment regimen. In 2015 Aprecia addressed

formulations

the combinations of chemical substances that make up a drug

this problem by creating a tablet that was designed to be easy to swallow. The drug, called Spritam, was also the first 3D-printed drug available to the public. Spritam is an antiseizure medication prescribed for people with epilepsy. "As we explored potential applications for our 3D printing technology in prescription drug products," says Don Wetherhold, chief executive officer of Aprecia, "it was important that we identified disease areas with a real need for patient-friendly forms of medication. Spritam . . . is the first in a line of products we are developing to provide patients and their caregivers with additional treatment options."[41]

To create Spritam, Aprecia developed ZipDose, an exclusive method of 3D printing. Based on research conducted at the Massachusetts Institute of Technology during the late 1990s, this technology does not use the multiton presses and dies of traditional drug manufacturing. The ZipDose printer is a powder based 3D ink-jet printer that measures about 6 feet by 12 feet (1.8 m by 3.6 m). To make the drug, the printer first deposits a powdered layer of Spritam's active pharmaceutical ingredient. Next, drops of liquid are sprayed onto the powder, binding the particles together in preparation for the next layer. This process is repeated several times until a complete tablet has been formed layer by layer. The resulting drug is a rough-surfaced, highly porous pill. When taken with just a sip of water, Spritam dissolves in the mouth in a matter of seconds, quickly allowing the required dose to be easily ingested. "By combining 3D [printing] technology with a highly-prescribed epilepsy treatment," Wetherhold notes, "Spritam is designed to fill a need for patients who struggle with their current medication experience."[42]

As of 2017, Spritam was the only 3D-printed drug approved by the Food and Drug Administration (FDA), the government agency that regulates the safety and effectiveness of consumer goods, including cosmetics, food, and drugs in the United States. As Aprecia plans to expand its line of 3D-printed drugs, other pharmaceutical companies are also exploring the uses of 3D technology. GlaxoSmithKline (GSK), one of the largest pharmaceutical manufacturers in the world, is one such company. "One of the areas we are exploring," says Martin Wallace, GSK's director of technology, "is whether we can print patient-specific dosage forms. Printing tailored medicine could simplify our supply chain dramatically." In 2016 the company held a 3D printing competition among its employees to encourage new uses for the technology. "We started to see ideas that we'd never considered and applications where 3D printing could be of benefit,"[43] says Wallace.

From Factory to Pharmacy to Home

The real work (and expense) in drug manufacturing comes in the development stages and the approval process. Once the drug goes into production, that process is relatively straightforward. The final step is to ship it to various pharmacies to be available when a patient brings in a doctor's prescription to be filled. However, it may be possible in the future for a drug created by 3D printing to be manufactured not in a factory but rather in a local pharmacy, at a hospital, or even in a doctor's office.

Microfish

Microfish cannot be found on a restaurant's menu, but sometime in the future they could be swimming around inside a person's bloodstream. And they just might save that person's life.

Engineers at the University of California, San Diego (UCSD), have created tiny 3D-printed microrobots that are shaped like fish and can swim in liquids. And they are indeed remarkably tiny. "We have developed an entirely new method to engineer nature-inspired microscopic swimmers that have complex geometric structures and are smaller than the width of a human hair," says Wei Zhu, a nanoengineering student at UCSD. The fish were created using a special high-resolution 3D printing technology called microscale continuous optical printing, which uses ultraviolet light instead of standard print heads. And as small as they are, the microfish contain even tinier elements—nanoparticles—that allow them to propel themselves and to be controlled by a magnetic field.

The medical uses of these microfish are just beginning to be explored. When injected into the human bloodstream, the fish can sense toxins in the blood and detoxify them, glowing red in the process. They could also be used as a drug delivery system or possibly even operate as precision surgical tools. Although the fish resemble minuscule sharks, other shapes could be printed. "With our 3D printing technology," explains Wei, "we are not limited to just fish shapes. We can rapidly build microrobots inspired by other biological organisms such as birds."

Quoted in Jacobs School of Engineering, "These Microscopic Fish Are 3D Printed to Do More than Swim," University of California, San Diego, August 25, 2015. www.jacobsschool.ucsd.edu.

There are advantages to having pharmacies 3D print their own medications. Bonnie Scott, a lawyer specializing in health and life sciences, sees the potential in such a future:

> 3-D printing could allow pharmacists to adapt medication doses specifically to patient needs (such as age, race, gender) and adjust those doses as needed. It also opens the door for producing new formulations of drugs, which could be particularly helpful for patients with multiple conditions. For example, a pharmacist could make one pill with multiple active ingredients. Reducing the amount of pills a patient has to take from ten to one may significantly improve medication compliance.[44]

Continued improvements in 3D printers might one day make it possible for people to print their own prescription drugs using recipes supplied by a lab. But this also has risks, including mistakes and using the technology for illicit purposes.

Although the idea of a local pharmacy printing medications for their customers may seem like a practical advancement, some forward-thinking theorists have taken the concept one step further, in which ordinary people have a 3D pharmaceutical printer in their home. Lee Cronin, a chemistry professor at Glasgow University in Scotland, has been on the cutting edge of research into using 3D printing in the fields of chemistry and medicine. "What Apple did for music," he explains, "I'd like to do for the discovery and distribution of prescription drugs."[45] As iPods bring music into the home, Cronin envisions 3D printers there also:

> Imagine your printer like a refrigerator that is full of all the ingredients you might require to make any dish. . . . If you apply that idea to making drugs, you have all your ingredients and you follow a recipe that a drug company gives

you. They will have validated that recipe in their lab. And when you have downloaded it and enabled the printer to read the software it will work. The value is in the recipe, not in the manufacture. It is an app, essentially.[46]

For those who are too sick or otherwise unable to go to a pharmacy, printing drugs at home would be a significant advantage, even if it is a long way down the road to becoming a reality. But with the ability to print drugs at home comes the risk of people creating illegal drugs or inadvertently making a dangerous formulation due to their lack of chemical knowledge.

The Dark Side of Printing Drugs

Law enforcement authorities have expressed concern over the ability of someone to 3D print something as dangerous as a working gun. Guns can be printed using 3D technology, but the process is tedious and the end result is a weapon of limited usefulness. In the pharmaceutical field, similar fears about the possibility of printing dangerous illicit drugs have also arisen.

Part of Cronin's research is his modification of a 3D printer into what he has dubbed the *chemputer*—essentially an entire chemistry set. "Nearly all drugs are made of carbon, hydrogen and oxygen," Cronin explains, "as well as readily available agents such as vegetable oils and paraffin. With a printer it should be possible that with a relatively small number of inks you can make any organic molecule."[47] Such a molecule might become part of a medicine that saves thousands of lives; yet in the wrong hands, it could be made into an illicit drug that can harm or kill even more.

Even without malicious intent, 3D-printed drugs can present serious problems. Pharmaceutical companies must run numerous clinical trials to confirm a new drug's safety and effectiveness. Results of these tests are submitted to the FDA for review, and its approval is required for the company to make the drug available to the public. Although this is standard procedure in the pharmaceutical industry, it would be impossible to perform such rigorous reviews on a drug printed at home, or even in a hospital or pharmacy, on a 3D printer. For David Hodgson, an attorney specializing in health care, numerous questions still need answers: "The current global, regional and local regulatory environment is incapable of accommodating the ambiguity of a 3D printing process. The question is are we regulating the printer as a medical device, the ingredients, or the person or organization doing the printing as the manufacturer and distributor?"[48]

Without such safeguards, the quality of drugs 3D printed outside of the large pharmaceutical companies could not be guaranteed and could lead to medicines that are ineffective at best and harmful at worst. Errors in drug formulation and the possibility of hackers tampering with 3D printing software could result in toxic drugs rather than beneficial ones. 3D printers can malfunction, extrusion nozzles can become dirty, and temperatures of the printing ingredients may not be properly regulated, all of which can affect the quality of a printed drug. Finally, unscrupulous hackers could steal a pharmaceutical company's drug formula and use 3D printers to create counterfeit drugs, sell them abroad, and place the reputation and financial position of the original manufacturer at considerable risk.

Asked when the ability to print drugs at home would become a reality, Cronin answered "maybe ten to fifteen years. Who knows?"[49] The fact is, nobody really knows when it will happen—if it happens at all. That leaves time for those charged with public safety to address these types of concerns.

The Advantages of 3D-Printed Drugs

Of course, printing drugs with 3D technology also has significant benefits. One of these is the ability to more precisely control medication dosages. According to Alvaro Goyanes, the founder of biotech company FabRx, "Tablets with precise personalized doses can be printed on-demand by pharmaceutical companies or even at hospitals or home health agencies to administer to patients at the point of care. I believe 3D printing can play a critical role in helping the pharmaceutical industry address the needs of personalized medicine."[50]

Dosage control is especially important for children. Prescribing the proper dosages is challenging for doctors, and it is not possible for pharmacies to keep numerous formulations of drugs on hand for the various ages and weights of children. An additional factor is a child's reluctance to take his or her medicine.

"Children don't like taking medicine," says Simon Gaisford, the head of pharmaceutics at University College London. "Now, in principle, we could ask a child, 'What's your favorite animal?' and print the tablet in any shape and color they like."[51] After all, what child would be reluctant to take a pill that has been printed in the shape of a dinosaur or superhero?

Shape is also a consideration when formulating drugs for adults. Tablets now come in just a few shapes, usually round or oval, due to the limitations of current manufacturing practices. But 3D printers can make drugs in any shape, from cubes to pyramids to spheres. Studies have found a connection between the shape of a pill and the way it releases medicine in the body.

Drug manufacturers are working with 3D printers to test different pill shapes. The goal is to more precisely time the release rate of medication—something that might be possible by creating pills of different shapes.

In practical terms, for example, where as one patient needs a fast-acting drug, another requires the same drug in a slower, timed-release manner. By printing tablets of the drug in different shapes, the release rate of the medicine can be precisely controlled for individual patients.

Multinozzle 3D printers are used to create tablets in which several different APIs are deposited, allowing different drugs with varying release times to be combined in a single pill. Some of these pills resemble a capsule embedded within an outer shell, but others are created in layers. As many as five different drugs have been incorporated in a 3D-printed tablet. The problem of orphan drugs is another area in which 3D printing is poised to become an important solution. An orphan drug is one that research has identified as a promising remedy for treating rare ailments, but its market is so small that

3D-Printed Help for Diabetics

More than 29 million Americans are living with diabetes, a chronic disease that impairs the body's production of the hormone insulin, which can cause serious complications. There are two kinds of diabetes: type 1, in which the body produces no insulin, and type 2, in which the body's insulin is not used properly.

3D printing is being used to help diabetics manage their disease. In 2015 researchers at Ohio State University began exploring 3D printing as a new way to make glucose sensors, which are inserted under the skin as part of insulin pumps often used by type 1 diabetics. A type of high-resolution 3D printing called electrohydrodynamic jet (E-jet) printing was used to make the sensors, which are less expensive to make and more comfortable for patients than standard sensors.

Many type 2 diabetics must monitor their glucose level several times a day with an external meter that uses expensive, nonreusable test strips. A student at Arizona State University has developed a prototype of a 3D-printed test strip that is less expensive than commercially available strips. Eventually, this could lead to diabetics printing their own test strips at home, promoting better compliance with the testing regimen.

it is not economically practical for a pharmaceutical company to manufacture. Using 3D printing to make small batches of orphan drugs could lower the cost and allow people with rare diseases a chance to receive much-needed medications.

A Disruptive Technology

3D printing's astounding potential for improving people's lives is so revolutionary that it has joined the ranks of advances called disruptive technology. The term is used to describe a radical innovation that replaces established technology, creates new markets, and reverberates through entire industries. Examples of such advances are many: the cell phone revolutionized the telecommunications industry, the personal computer changed the way people work, and the Internet altered nearly every aspect of daily life. The 3D printing of drugs can almost certainly be added to this list, as it may be a harbinger of a radical change in the trillion-dollar drug industry. "3D printing," says software consultant David Hess, "has a true potential to disrupt the generic pharmaceutical supply chain, giving local pharmacies and hospitals the ability to create their own medicines. API suppliers could ship directly to those endpoints, shipping to regions where their consumers will have their drugs rendered."[52]

As a disruptive technology, 3D-printed pharmaceuticals may not be a bad thing if they allow more people to receive medication more efficiently and at a lower cost. Just as the Internet changed the way people live, 3D-printed drugs may help individuals live longer and healthier lives.

CHAPTER 5

3D Printing in Surgery and Research

In early 2015, Dr. Redmond Burke was losing sleep over an upcoming surgery he was to perform. The patient, five-year-old Mia Gonzalez, was having difficulty breathing due to a congenital heart problem. Mia had a double aortic arch, which created an abnormality called a vascular ring that wrapped around Mia's trachea, making it difficult for her to breathe. Heart surgery is always demanding, but it would be even more so in Mia's case due not only to her age but also to the nature of her condition. "She had one of the rarest versions of a rare problem," notes Burke. "Because of that, people make mistakes when they encounter her heart defect."[53] Burke was determined not to make a mistake in Mia's case, and he used a 3D printer to help ensure that outcome.

At Nicklaus Children's Hospital in Miami, Florida, where Burke was supervising Mia's case, he first had a magnetic resonance imaging (MRI) scan made of Mia's heart. Then, the information from the scan was fed into the hospital's new 3D printer, which created a model of Mia's heart. "For a heart surgeon," says Burke, "I'm used to being able to hold a heart when I operate on it. But I can't hold an MRI in my hands and feel it and create an operation. The 3D-printed heart gives you a fantastic view of a very complex, three-dimensional problem."[54]

Burke studied the model for weeks, even carrying it around in his gym bag so he could show it to colleagues and ask for suggestions. Eventually he determined the best way to proceed and prepared his surgical team for the operation. Using the model, he explained the surgery to Mia's family and showed them how he would repair the heart defect.

After studying the model, Burke knew exactly where he needed to place the incision; because of this, he could make it smaller and less painful and ensure a faster recovery time for Mia. After successful surgery in May 2015, Mia quickly recovered and was finally able to run and jump like any other five-year-old. But she has one thing few other children have: the 3D model of her heart, which she keeps as a souvenir.

3D Surgical Models

Mia was one of about twenty pediatric patients at Nicklaus Children's Hospital who, by the end of 2015, had benefited from models made using the hospital's 3D printer. The practice of

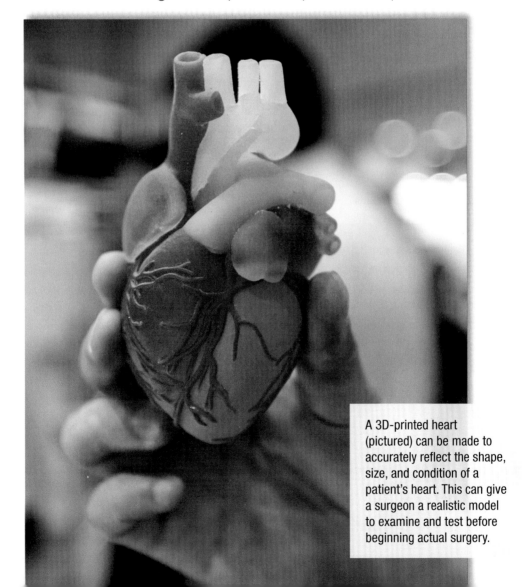

A 3D-printed heart (pictured) can be made to accurately reflect the shape, size, and condition of a patient's heart. This can give a surgeon a realistic model to examine and test before beginning actual surgery.

making 3D printed surgical models is continuing to grow, in part due to the inherent limitations of using information provided by such 2D media as MRI and computed tomography scans for reference during surgery. Chief engineer Jimmie Beacham of GE Healthcare Research in Wisconsin explains:

> All humans are built a little bit differently. When a surgeon has to go in and do a procedure, they are sometimes surprised by what they find. Surgeons sometimes have to repeatedly go to a workstation, look at the image on the screen and try to figure out what's going on. It slows the surgery down and increases the odds of introducing infection or slowing the patient's recovery time.[55]

aneurysm

a weak spot in an artery that, if ruptured, can cause serious injury or death

photopolymer

a plastic that exhibits a change when exposed to light and is often used as a material in 3D printing

With 3D-printed models as a reference, surgeons can anticipate complications that may arise during surgery and find solutions even before the patient is wheeled into the operating room. For example, surgeons in a hospital in Japan who were preparing to transplant an adult liver into a child needed to know how to fit the larger organ into the child's smaller space. By making a 3D model of the liver and cutting away sections with a scalpel, they determined exactly how to fit the actual liver into the child. In Buffalo, New York, Teresa Flint entered a hospital suffering from a brain aneurysm, a weak spot in an artery that would likely be fatal if it ruptured. Surgeons made several attempts to repair the aneurysm, but they failed each time. Fortunately, those attempts were made not on Flint but rather on a 3D model of the aneurysm. Printed with an $87,000 Stratasys printer, the model was made of a flexible photopolymer that replicated the texture and feel of the real structure and even had blood flowing through it during presurgical tests. The printed model was accurate to 0.0005 inches (.013 mm).

Practicing on the 3D model, surgeon Adnan Siddiqui learned that his first choice of treatment—placing a metal device in the artery to block blood flow to the aneurysm—was unworkable. "Our original plan," he recalls, "was to treat her aneurysm with a metallic basket—delivered into the area with a tiny tube. After attempting the procedure on the 3D printed replica, we realized it just wasn't going to work."[56] After trying several other surgical options on the model, Siddiqui finally came up with a workable solution. The surgery took about forty-five minutes, much less

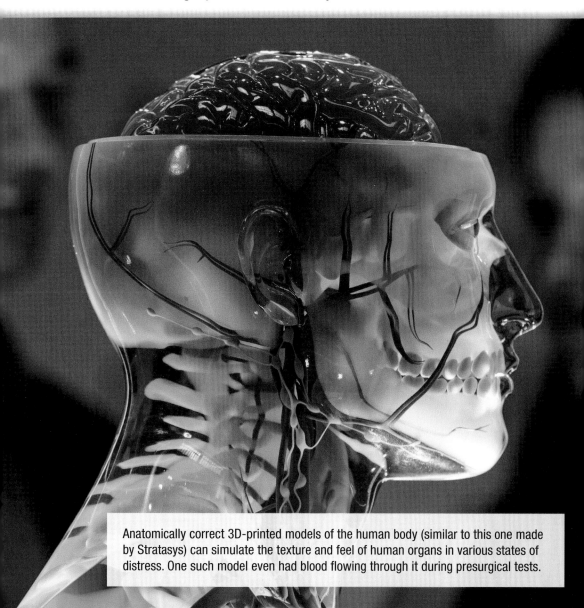

Anatomically correct 3D-printed models of the human body (similar to this one made by Stratasys) can simulate the texture and feel of human organs in various states of distress. One such model even had blood flowing through it during presurgical tests.

than the normal three to four hours for such a delicate and complicated procedure. Flint's successful surgery was largely due to the doctor's ability to try different surgical options on the 3D model. The future should see more such positive outcomes as 3D printing becomes further established as a valuable technology in hospitals. One day, Siddiqui predicts, "this is going to become the standard of care in complicated elective cases where you have time to see what strategies will work."[57]

Education for Medical Students

Before doctors like Siddiqui step into an actual operating room, they spend years in medical school learning anatomy, physiolo-

Surgical Tools on Mars

With the possibility of creating a human colony on Mars looming in the not-too-distant future, a group of researchers called Mars Without Borders (MWOB) is preparing for that eventuality. They are working on ways to use 3D printing for medical purposes in the hostile environment of space.

In 2014 MWOB members at Utah's Mars Desert Research Station studied how solar-powered 3D printers could be used in telesurgery, which involves nonmedical personnel performing operations guided by doctors on Earth. The simulation included the use of 3D-printed surgical tools. Among those tools were a scalpel handle and a finger splint. In addition, a unique claw was designed to be attached to the glove of a spacesuit. Although looking more like an elongated fingernail than a surgical instrument, the claw was useful in such medical tasks as peeling open a packaged bandage to cover a wound. "It is really feasible to imagine use of 3D printing technology, especially solar powered 3D printers and their uses for creating 3D printed surgical tools and other medical instruments for future Martian settlers," remark Matteo Borri and Dr. Susan Jewell of MWOB. "There will always be a need for medical care especially [when there is] the urgent need to have immediate access to surgical and medical interventions to save the life of the injured astronaut or sick crew." From the deserts of Utah, the next step may be the surface of Mars itself.

Quoted in Eddie Krassenstein, "Solar Powered 3D Printers on Mars? Researchers Successfully Test Feasibility of Printing Surgical Tools on Red Planet," 3DPrint.com, January 22, 2015. https://3dprint.com.

gy, biochemistry, and other medical and scientific subjects. For medical students, acquiring this knowledge begins with reading numerous books containing thousands of facts to be learned, memorized, and recalled at test time. Someone once jokingly stated, "Whoever learns anatomy only from books, should only operate on books."[58] Of course, medical students learn in other ways as well, from attending lectures to clinical practice. With the advent of 3D printing technology, physicians-in-training now have another source for gaining medical knowledge.

"The way we see, understand and then interpret human anatomy for teaching and inevitably for patient care has changed," says Craig Goodmurphy, a professor of pathology and anatomy at Eastern Virginia Medical School (EVMS). Goodmurphy uses 3D-printed models in his anatomy classes. "We have the opportunity," he says, "to create models that are specific to complicated pathology, and we can do it in a more cost-effective way."[59] 3D printing is not only a science but also an art, says consultant Miro Kirov, a sculptor who creates intricate 3D anatomical models for EVMS. "This is the fusion of art and science, with the added complexity of the human form. I must find every intricate detail, every curve and turn, and then teach the printer how to create it."[60]

3D printers have been used to create accurate fetal skeletons, which are embedded in a substance that simulates the human uterine environment. Students then practice their skills in using ultrasound scanners to determine the size and position of the fetus as well as to detect abnormalities. In ophthalmology classes, life-size eyes can be printed and filled with gel to represent the fluid inside the eyeball. Suturing and diagnostic skills can be practiced over and over on these models without the expense of using eyes from human cadavers (bodies donated for medical instruction) or animals.

Using cadavers for medical training has been a standard procedure for centuries. But storing them properly is expensive, and medical schools must often cope with problems of availability. To solve these problems, Monash University in Australia used scans of human X-rays and cadavers to develop a kit that contains 3D-printed anatomical body parts. As a result, 3D models of virtually any part of the human body can be ordered and printed in

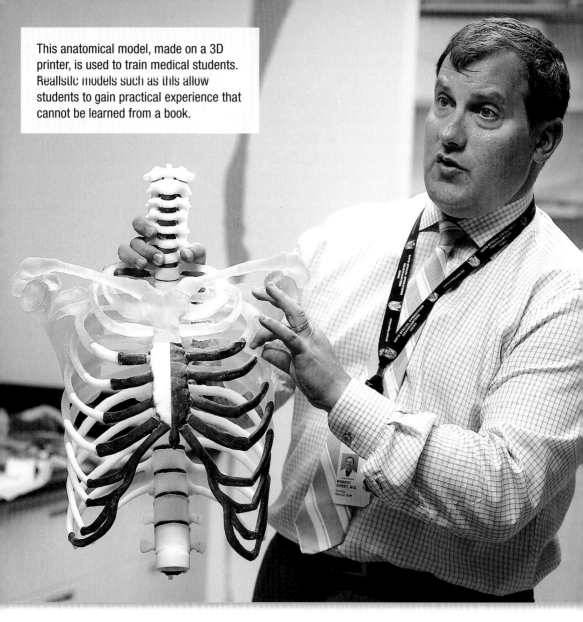

This anatomical model, made on a 3D printer, is used to train medical students. Realistic models such as this allow students to gain practical experience that cannot be learned from a book.

anatomically accurate colors. According to professor Paul McMenamin at Monash University,

> We believe our kit will revolutionize learning for medical students by enabling them to look inside the body and see the muscles, tendons, ligaments, and blood vessels. At the moment it can be incredibly hard for students to understand the three dimensional form of human anatomy, and we believe this kit will make a huge difference—a sort of 3D textbook.[61]

Actual textbooks will always remain an integral part of medical education. But with the addition of new tools like 3D printing, that education can only become better for both the students and their future patients.

Tools for the Surgeon

As 3D printing has become a valuable tool in the medical school classroom, it has also become a source for many of the tools that doctors use in surgery and other medical procedures. A surgery involves many different types of instruments: scalpels and scissors for cutting, hemostats for clamping blood vessels, retractors to provide access to the operating field, and numerous other specialized implements. Although surgical instruments are usually made of stainless steel, plastic instruments are now being created with ordinary 3D printers.

In 2013 at the University of Arizona, researchers used a MakerBot Replicator 2 3D printer to create a prototype surgical tool called an army-navy retractor. A simple U-shaped instrument, the retractor was made from polylactic acid, a plastic that has been proved safe for surgical use. It measured about 6.7 inches (17 cm) long and took about ninety minutes to print. The resulting instrument was found to be sturdy enough for operating room use and handled sterilization with no problems. Researchers estimated that the cost of printing the army-navy retractor was a mere forty-six cents.

Along with retractors, specialized tools are often required for delicate surgical procedures. One such procedure is repairing a tear in the anterior cruciate ligament (ACL) of the knee, which is among the most common injuries in professional sports. ACL operations often fail after surgery because of stress on the graft inserted to repair the ligament. Orthopedic surgeon Dana Piasecki realized that the standard use of a straight drill instead of a flexible one during surgery was the problem. Piasecki concluded that he "needed a tool that could be inserted into the inner knee space to grasp the flexible drill, steer it to the proper spot on the femur and hold it during the drilling process."[62] Piasecki created that tool with a 3D printer, first as a plastic prototype and then with a strong metal alloy called Inconel 718. It worked so well that Piasecki patented the instrument and began marketing it under tho namo Pathfindor ACL Guide. It has produced a 95 percent success rate in preventing the need for repeat ACL surgery, and it costs about 97 percent less than if manufactured using traditional methods.

Other 3D-printed medical instruments owe their existence to origami, the Japanese art of paper folding. In most surgeries, doctors strive to make their incisions as small as possible, but this is not always feasible due to manufacturing limits on the size of instruments currently available. Engineers at Brigham Young University (BYU) in Provo, Utah, are challenging these limits with 3D printers that can create instruments able to go through an incision as small as 0.1 inches (3 mm). Incisions that small usually heal without the need for sutures. "We'd like something to get quite small to go through the incision, but once it's inside, we'd like

Fighting Cancer with 3D Printing

One of the most feared diseases is cancer, which claimed more than half a million American lives in 2016. Researchers are now using 3D-printed models of tumors to help in the fight against this deadly disease. At a university in Scotland, researchers are printing 3D models of brain tumors to study how these rogue cells grow in the body. According to Nicholas Leslie of Heriot-Watt University in Edinburgh,

> We have developed a novel 3D printing technique to print brain tumor cells for the first time, cells that continue to grow rapidly, more closely mimicking the growth of these aggressive tumors in real life. Our goal is that this should provide a new way of testing drugs to treat brain tumors, leading to new treatments and speeding up the process by which new drugs become available to patients.

The scientists print the models using cells taken from a patient's tumor to mimic the tumor's growth in real life, something that cells grown in a laboratory cannot do. The project is designed to help researchers study how the cells react to various drugs, which would allow them to create more effective courses of therapy. Leslie's colleague, Will Shu, hopes that their "research will help develop a model that closely matches . . . the response of individuals' brain tumors to drugs, allowing more effective treatment to be carried out for patients."

Quoted in Greg Russell, "3D Printing Is New Tool in Bid to Fight Brain Cancer," *National*, May 24, 2015. www.thenational.scot.

it to get much larger," says BYU engineering professor Spencer Magleby. Taking their cue from the intricate folds of origami, the BYU team developed the D-Core, an instrument that begins flat but unfolds into two rounded surfaces after it is inserted through an incision. 3D printing allows these tiny tools to be made simpler, with fewer moving parts. "These small instruments will allow for a whole new range of surgeries to be performed—hopefully one day manipulating things as small as nerves," Magleby says. "The origami-inspired ideas really help us to see how to make things smaller and smaller and to make them simpler and simpler."[63]

3D Printing in Medical Research

Along with surgical tools, 3D printing has been used to create tools for testing new pharmaceuticals. The current US drug testing process is expensive, and many people oppose using animals for such tests. Research analyst Madhumitha Rangesa notes that "using 3D-printed tissues for drug testing, clinical trials and toxicity testing will have a huge impact in the pharmaceutical sector, as they will help eliminate costly animal testing and use of synthetic tissues."[64]

Gabor Forgacs understands the value of 3D printing in drug trials. He has worked with pharmaceutical companies in building 3D-printed organoids, or miniature organs, for use in drug testing:

> We take human liver cells and we build a 3D little teeny tiny liver that still can be maintained in culture and we tell [pharmaceutical companies], OK, why don't you try the drug on the 3D human structure and if the drug does not work and the little liver dies, well then don't go any further because chances are that when you put it into a human, it's not going to work.[65]

Building a full-size organ, such as a heart, for researchers to study is an impossibly complex task. Harvard University's Wyss Institute has come up with a 3D-printed alternative that it calls a heart-on-a-chip. Looking more like a computer chip than an actual heart, the heart-on-a-chip beats like a real heart, permitting tests to be performed without the need for a living organ. It was created using a fully automated 3D printer that simultaneously dispenses six different inks. Sensors embedded in the chip allow measurement of the electrical and mechanical properties of the tiny organ as it beats. As Wyss research associate Johan Lind explains, "These integrated sensors allow researchers to continuously collect data while tissues mature and improve their contractility [the ability of a muscle to shorten, or contract]. Similarly, they will enable studies of gradual effects of chronic exposure to toxins."[66] The data collected from the heart-on-a-chip will help in understanding the way the human heart works and how it reacts to disease.

The heart-on-a-chip is part of a class of research tools called microphysiological systems (MPS). In the past, the Wyss Institute has produced several MPS chips simulating the lungs, intestines, kidneys, and tongue. But creating these one at a time using traditional methods was expensive and time-consuming, and accurate test results were difficult to obtain. With 3D printing, these problems are eliminated, and the prospect of economical mass-producing of new MPS chips becomes a possibility. Wyss Institute researchers hope to eventually produce ten 3D-printed organs-on-a-chip and link them together to create a virtual human body that can be used for various testing applications.

> **microphysiological**
>
> relating to the functions of living organisms on a very small scale

Although the heart is a relatively simple organ, the brain is infinitely more complex, with 100 billion nerve cells working to keep the body functioning. It is this complexity that makes it difficult for researchers to unravel the brain's mysteries. "It's the 21st century and we still don't know how the brain works,"[67] comments engineering professor Stan Skafidas. Yet 3D printing has lessened the difficulty of studying the brain. A team of researchers from universities in Australia and Texas has created a 3D model of the layered structure that makes up the human brain by using a gel-like substance infused with brain cells as bioink. Before the advent of 3D printing, the study of the brain was limited to using animal brains, human cadavers, or 2D media. A 3D printer can create a layered representation of brain structures, giving scientists a more accurate representation of the six layers of the human brain. According to professor Gordon Wallace, a member of the research team, "Looking at what's going on in 3D—in a similar structure to the real human brain—will give us a much better idea of the biology behind neurodegenerative diseases like Alzheimer's and Parkinson's disease, and help researchers working on ways to treat them."[68]

neurodegenerative

a disease that has a damaging effect on the function of nerves, especially in the brain

Whether in university medical research laboratories, factories creating prosthetics and drugs, or hospital operating rooms, 3D printing's place in the future of health care is all but certain. What once seemed a part of science fiction has evolved into a reality that holds the potential to benefit people's lives and health and to ensure the continued well-being of generations to come.

SOURCE NOTES

Introduction: A Revolution in Medicine

1. Glenn Green, "Saving a Baby's Life with a 3D Laser Printer: Kaiba's Story," *Hail to the Little Victors* (blog), University of Michigan Health System, May 22, 2013. www.uofmhealth blogs.org.

2. Quoted in Peter Mellgard, "3D Printing Will 'Enable a New Kind of Future,'" *Huffington Post*. www.huffingtonpost.com.

3. Yu Shrike Zhang, "Bioprinting: The Future of Medicine," 3DMedNet, May 19, 2017. www.3dmednet.com.

4. Quoted in Amir Khan, "How 3-D Printing Will Revolutionize Prosthetics," *US News & World Report*, July 16, 2014. www.usnews.com.

5. Quoted in Mellgard, "3D Printing Will 'Enable a New Kind of Future.'"

Chapter 1: The Evolution of 3D Printing

6. Ivan Sutherland, *Sketchpad: A Man-Machine Graphical Communication System*. Cambridge, UK: University of Cambridge Computer Laboratory, technical report, no. 574, September 2003, p. 17.

7. Quoted in Matthew Sparkes, "We Laughed, We Cried, We Stayed Up All Night Imagining," *Telegraph* (London), June 18, 2014. www.telegraph.co.uk.

8. Quoted in Matthew Ponsford and Nick Glass, "The Night I Invented 3D Printing," CNN, February 14, 2014. www.cnn.com.

9. Quoted in Ponsford and Glass, "The Night I Invented 3D Printing."

10. Quoted in Chanpory Rith, "What Michelangelo Can Teach You About Good Design," *LifeClever* (blog), January 29, 2008. www.lifeclever.com.

11. Quoted in Jamie Gooch, "Point-Counterpoint: Additive vs. Subtractive Rapid Prototyping," RapidReady Technology, September 3, 2013. www.rapidreadytech.com.

12. Quoted in Neil Mohr, "The 3D Printers That Print Themselves: How RepRap Will Change the World," Tech Radar, July 1, 2014. www.techradar.com.

13. Quoted in Travis Hessman, "Take 5: Q&A with Chuck Hull, Co-founder, 3D Systems," *Industry Week,* November 6, 2013. www.industryweek.com.

Chapter 2: Replacing Organs

14. Quoted in Dan Lieberman and Ely Brown, "The Waiting Game: 9 Organ Transplant Patients Fight to Survive," *Nightline*, ABC News, May 1, 2012. www.abcnews.go.com.

15. Quoted in Anthony Atala, "Printing a Human Kidney," TED Talk, March 2011. www.ted.com.

16. Anthony Atala, "Growing New Organs," TED Talk, January 2010. www.ted.com.

17. Atala, "Printing a Human Kidney."

18. Quoted in Atala, "Printing a Human Kidney."

19. Quoted in Carey Goldberg, "Doctors Grow Bladder Cells and Produce Rebuilt Organ," *Boston Globe*, April 4, 2006. www.boston.com.

20. Quoted in ScienceDaily, "Researcher Uses Bioprinter to Print Three-Dimensional Cellular Structures," February 18, 2004. www.sciencedaily.com.

21. Gabor Forgacs, "On-Demand Body Parts: Inventing the Bio-Printer," *All Things Considered*, National Public Radio, March 14, 2010. www.npr.org.

22. Quoted in Forrest K. Lewis, "Wyss Institute Team Reveals New Bioprinting Technique," *Harvard Crimson*, February 24, 2014. www.thecrimson.com.

23. Quoted in Lydialyle Gibson, "Building Toward a Kidney: Jennifer Lewis's Quest to Advance 3-D Organ Printing," *Harvard Magazine*, January/February 2017. www.harvardmagazine.com.

24. Quoted in Lizette Borelli, "Chinese Girl Becomes World's First to Receive Full Skull Reconstruction via 3D Printing," Medical Daily, July 16, 2015. www.medicaldaily.com.

25. Quoted in Bridget Butler Millsaps, "Thanks to Denver's 3D Printing Store, DU Is 3D Printing Heart Valves, Ears & More," 3DPrint.com, March 3, 2016. https://3dprint.com.

26. Quoted in Millsaps, "Thanks to Denver's 3D Printing Store, DU Is 3D Printing Heart Valves, Ears & More."

27. Quoted in Brandon Griggs, "The Next Frontier in 3-D Printing: Human Organs," CNN, April 5, 2014. www.cnn.com.

Chapter 3: Creating New Body Parts

28. Quoted in Create Prosthetics, "Create Prosthetics Makes the First Medical-Grade 3D-printed Prosthetic Arm," Create O&P, June 23, 2016. www.createoandp.com.

29. Quoted in Jeremy Simon, "A $50 3D-Printed Prosthesis Compared to a $42,000 Myoelectric Prosthesis (3D Universe)," YouTube. www.youtube.com.

30. Quoted in Ian Birrell, "Could 3D Printing Revolutionize Prosthetic Limbs and Care for Amputees?," Independent (London), February 20, 2017. www.independent.co.uk.

31. Quoted in James Vincent, "3D Printing: How a $100 Arm Is Giving Hope to Sudan's 50,000 War Amputees," Independent (London), January 20, 2014. www.independent.co.uk.

32. Quoted in Julia Burpee, "Canadian Team Uses 3D Printer to Make Artificial Legs for Ugandans," CBC News, February 16, 2015. www.cbc.ca.

33. Quoted in Burpee, "Canadian Team Uses 3D Printer to Make Artificial Legs for Ugandans."

34. Quoted in Ben Hobson, "Denise Schindler to Become World's First Paralympic Cyclist to Use 3D-Printed Prosthesis," Dezeen, May 12, 2016. www.dezeen.com.

35. Quoted in Hobson, "Denise Schindler to Become World's First Paralympic Cyclist to Use 3D-Printed Prosthesis."

36. Quoted in Nick Webster, "Amputee Horse Rider Gets First 3D-Printed Prosthetic Leg in UAE," National (Abu Dhabi), May 31, 2017. www.thenational.ae.

37. Quoted in Daniel Terdiman, "3D-Printed Exoskeleton Helps Paralyzed Skier Walk Again," CNET, February 18, 2014. www.cnet.com.

38. Amanda Boxtel, "3D-Printed Exoskeleton by Ekso Bionics and 3D Systems," YouTube, March 28, 2014. www.youtube.com.

39. Quoted in Mount Sinai Inside, "Using 3D Print Technology to Restore a Child's Nose," December 28, 2015. http://inside.mountsinai.org.

40. Quoted in Hanna Watkin, "Indian Woman Walks Again Thanks to 3D Printed Vertebrae," All About 3D Printing, February 23, 2017. www.all3dp.com.

Chapter 4: Printing Pharmaceuticals

41. Quoted in Aprecia Pharmaceuticals, "First FDA Approved Medicine Manufactured Using 3D Printing Technology Now Available," press release, March 22, 2016. www.aprecia.com/pdf/ApreciaSPRITAMLaunchPressRelease__FINAL.PDF.

42. Quoted in Christine Blank, "FDA Approves First 3D Epilepsy Drug," *Formulary Journal,* August 6, 2015. www.formularyjournal.modernmedicine.com.

43. Quoted in Michael Petch, "Just Say Whoa: GlaxoSmithKline and the Future of 3D-Printed Pharmaceuticals," *Redshift*, September 13, 2016. www.redshift.autodesk.com.

44. Quoted in Christina Farr, "Why 3D Printing Has 'Tremendous Potential' for Big Pharma," KQED Science, August 6, 2015. www.kqed.org.

45. Quoted in Jelmer Luimstra, "Why There Are Two Sides to 3D Printed Drugs," 3DPrinting.com, March 8, 2014. https://3dprinting.com.

46. Quoted in Tim Adams, "The 'Chemputer' That Could Print Out Any Drug," *Guardian* (Manchester, UK), July 21, 2012. www.theguardian.com.

47. Quoted in Steven Kotler, "Vice Wars: How 3D Printing Will Revolutionize Crime," *Forbes*, July 31, 2012. www.forbes.com.

48. Quoted in Ann Robinson, "Welcome to the Complex World of 3D-Printed Drugs," *Guardian* (Manchester, UK), August 21, 2015. www.theguardian.com.

49. Quoted in Kevin Holmes, "In the Future, Your Drug Dealer Will Be a Printer," *Vice,* July 4, 2012. www.vice.com.

50. Quoted in Ken Congdon, "3D Printing Poised to Make Big Pharma Impact," Pharmaceutical Online, June 3, 2015. www .pharmaceuticalonline.com.

51. Quoted in Bridget Butler Millsaps, "Researchers Complete Trial Run for 3D Printed Medication—Including Dinosaur Shapes for Finicky Kids," 3DPrint.com, June 16, 2015. https://3dprint.com.

52. Quoted in Pharmaceutical Manufacturing, "Q&A: 3D Technology Emerges," May 31, 2017. www.pharmamanufacturing.com.

Chapter 5: 3D Printing in Surgery and Research

53. Quoted in Andrew Zaleski, "How 3D Printing Saved a Five-Year-Old's Life," *Fortune*, October 7, 2015. www.fortune.com.

54. Quoted in Zaleski, "How 3D Printing Saved a Five-Year-Old's Life."

55. Quoted in Sarah Saunders, "GE Healthcare Researching Ways to 3D Print Medical Models with the Touch of a Button," 3DPrint.com, April 17, 2017. https://3dprint.com.

56. Quoted in *Robotics Trends* Staff, "3D Printing Helps Cure Woman's Brain Aneurysm," *Robotics Trends*. www.robotics trends.com.

57. Quoted in Henry L. Davis, "3D Printing Emerging as Significant Technology in Health Care," *Buffalo News,* December 2, 2015. www.buffalonews.com.

58. Quoted in John Graber, "Stratasys and University of Malaya Team Up to Create Surgical Biomodels," 3D Printer World, November 29, 2013. www.3dprinterworld.com.

59. Quoted in *EVMS Magazine,* "3D Printing," no. 8.5, 2015–2016. www.evms.edu.

60. Quoted in *EVMS Magazine,* "3D Printing."

61. Quoted in T.E. Halterman, "3D Printed Anatomy Series Released by Monash University: A Medical Training Game Changer," 3DPrint.com, May 27, 2015. https://3dprint.com.

62. Quoted in Clare Scott, "Orthopedic Surgeon Develops Game-Changing 3D Printed Tool for ACL Surgeries," 3DPrint.com, January 7, 2016. https://3dprint.com.

63. Quoted in Tom Hollingshead, "Tiny Origami-Inspired Devices Opening Up New Possibilities for Minimally-Invasive Surgery," BYU News, March 2, 2016. www.news.byu.edu.

64. Quoted in "New Research Reveals Impact of 3D Printing Technology in Medical Devices and Pharmaceutical Sector," News Medical, March 23, 2017. www.news-medical.net.

65. Quoted in Emily Spivack, "PopTech Interview: Gabor Forgacs on the Reality of 3D Organ Printing," PopTech, February 24, 2011. www.poptech.org.

66. Quoted in Beau Jackson, "3D Printing Advances End to Animal Testing with Harvard's Heart on a Chip," 3D Printing Industry, October 25, 2016. www.3dprintingindustry.com.

67. Quoted in Abdul Rehman, "Melbourne Researchers 3D Print Brain Tissue," 3D Print Headquarters, December 20, 2015. www.3dprinthq.com.

68. Quoted in ScienceDaily, "Studying Human Brain Using 3D Printing Technology," March 21, 2016. www.sciencedaily.com.

Books

Diane Ackerman, *The Human Age: The World Shaped by Us*. New York: Norton, 2014.

Liza Wallach Kloski, *Getting Started with 3D Printing: A Hands-on Guide to the Hardware, Software, and Services Behind the New Manufacturing Revolution*. San Francisco: Maker Media, 2016.

Hod Lipson and Melba Kurman, *Fabricated: The New World of 3D Printing*. Indianapolis: Wilet & Sons, 2013.

Hal Markovitz, *What Is the Future of 3D Printing?* San Diego: ReferencePoint, 2017.

Internet Sources

Benedict, "Crowd4Africa Raising €23K to Bring 3D Printers and 3D Printed Prostheses to African Hospitals," 3Ders.org, March 21, 2016. www.3ders.org/articles/20160321-crowd4africa-raising-23k-to-bring-3d-printers-and-3d-printed-prostheses-to-african-hospitals.html.

Economist, "Printing a Bit of Me," March 8, 2014. www.economist.com/news/technology-quarterly/21598322-bioprinting-building-living-tissue-3d-printer-becoming-new-business.

Hope King, "College Student 3D Prints His Own Braces," CNN Money, March 16, 2016. www.money.cnn.com/2016/03/16/technology/homemade-invisalign/index.html.

Steven Leckart, "How 3-D Printing Body Parts Will Revolutionize Medicine," *Popular Science*, August 6, 2013. www.popsci.com/science/article/2013-07/how-3-d-printing-body-parts-will-revolutionize-medicine.

Tanya Lewis, "7 Cool Uses of 3D Printing in Medicine," Live Science, February 4, 2013. www.livescience.com/26853-3d-printing-medicine.html.

Siena College, "Siena Students Create *Frozen*-Themed Prosthetic Arm for Nine-Year-Old Girl," June 29, 2016. www.siena.edu/news-events/article/siena-students-create-frozen-themed-prosthetic-arm-for-nine-year-old-girl.

Matthew Sparkes, "We Laughed, We Cried, We Stayed Up All Night Imagining," *Telegraph* (London), June 18, 2014. www.telegraph.co.uk/technology/news/10908560/We-laughed-we-cried-we-stayed-up-all-night-imagining.html.

Andrew Zaleski, "How 3D Printing Saved a 5-Year-Old's Life," *Fortune*, October 10, 2015. www.fortune.com/2015/10/07/3d-printing-saved-a-5-year-olds-life.

Websites

Enabling the Future (http://enablingthefuture.org). The website of e-NABLE, a volunteer community of individuals worldwide who use their 3D printers to create free 3D-printed prosthetics for those in need of an upper limb assistive device.

Organovo (http://organovo.com). This website for the pioneering company highlights its work in the field of medical 3D printing and describes the process it uses to create living tissues.

3D Forged (https://3dforged.com). This comprehensive website provides links to hundreds of online articles about 3D printing. It includes a chapter devoted to 3D printing in medicine and health care.

3D MedNet (www.3dmednet.com). This website is dedicated to presenting information on the medical uses of 3D printing. It includes links devoted to 3D printing news, videos, surgical applications, pharmaceuticals, and more.

3D Print (https://3dprint.com). A website covering the latest news about all aspects of 3D printing, including 3D design, manufacturing, research, and medical applications.

INDEX

PICTURE CREDITS

Craig E. Blohm has written numerous books and magazine articles for young readers. He and his wife, Desiree, reside in Tinley Park, Illinois.